INADMISSIBLE EVIDENCE

INADMISSIBLE EVIDENCE

A Play

by

JOHN OSBORNE

FABER AND FABER

London & Boston

First published in 1965
by Faber and Faber Limited
3 Queen Square London W.C.1
First published in this edition 1967
Reprinted 1969, 1974 and 1978
Printed in Great Britain by
Whitstable Litho Ltd., Whitstable, Kent
All rights reserved

ISBN 0 571 08177 0 (Faber Paperbacks)
ISBN 0 571 06174 5 (hard bound edition)

All professional inquiries in regard to this play should be addressed to the author's agent, Margery Vosper Ltd., 53a, Shaftesbury Avenue, London W.1, and all amateur inquiries should be addressed to Messrs. Evans Brothers Ltd., Montague House, Russell Square, London W.C.1

The first performance of *Inadmissible Evidence* was given at the Royal Court Theatre, Sloane Square, London, on September 9th, 1964, by the English Stage Company. It was directed by Antony Page, and the décor was by Jocelyn Herbert. The part of Bill Maitland was played by Nicol Williamson.

CAST

Bill Maitland

Hudson

Jones

Shirley

Joy

Mrs. Garnsey

Jane Maitland

Liz

ACT ONE

The location where a dream takes place. A site of helplessness, of oppression and polemic. The structure of this particular dream is the bones and dead objects of a Solicitor's Office. It has a desk, files, papers, dust, books, leather armchairs, a large, Victorian coat stand, and the skeleton of an outer office with clerks, girls and a telephonist. Downstage is a DOCK *in which stands the prisoner of this dream,* BILL MAITLAND. *At back, high above the outer office, hangs the Royal Coat of Arms. In front of this are the green benches of one of the High Courts of Justice, in which sits one of* HER MAJESTY'S JUDGES. *From centre a* CLERK *of the* COURT *reads the indictment. Before this there has been an air of floating inertia before the three actors come to some sort of life out of the blur of dream.*

CLERK: William Henry Maitland, you are accused of
having unlawfully and wickedly published and
made known, and caused to be procured and
made
known, a wicked, bawdy and scandalous object.
Intending—

BILL: Object?

JUDGE: Proceed, proceed.

CLERK: Object. Intending to vitiate and corrupt the
morals of the liege subjects of our Lady the
Queen, to debauch and poison the minds of
divers of the liege subjects of our Lady and to

raise and create in them lustful desires, and to bring the liege subjects into a state of wickedness, lewdness and debauchery. How do you plead? Guilty or Not Guilty?

BILL: Not guilty.

(*Pause.*)

CLERK: Place your right hand on the book and repeat after me: I swear by Almighty God—

BILL: I swear. . . . My Lord, I wish to affirm.

JUDGE: Very well.

CLERK: Do you swear and affirm?

BILL: I swear and affirm. . . . (*Pause. Then a hoarse rattle. Clearing his throat at intervals.*) I hereby swear and affirm. Affirm. On my. . . . Honour? By my belief. My belief in . . . in . . . the technological revolution, the pressing, growing, pressing, urgent need for more and more scientists, and more scientists, for more and more

schools and universities and universities and schools, the theme

of change, realistic decisions based on a highly developed and professional study of society by people who really know their subject, the overdue need for us to adapt ourselves to different conditions, the theme and challenge of such rapid change, change, rapid change. (*Flails. The* JUDGE *looks at him reassuringly and he picks up again.*) In the ninety seven per cent, ninety seven, of all the scientists who have ever lived in the history of the world since the days of Euclid, Pythagoras and Archimedes. Who, who are alive and at work today, today, now, at this time, in the inevitability of automation and the ever increasing need, need, oh, need

10

for, the stable ties of modern family life, rethinking, reliving, making way for the motor car, forty million by nineteen; in a forward looking, outward looking, programme controlled machine tool line reassessment. With, yes, with faculties of memory and judgement far beyond the capacity of any human grief, being. Or any group of human who has ever lived. (*Pause.*)

JUDGE: Yes?

BILL: In the facts, above all the facts, inescapable. Anna, my wife, Hudson, I mean my managing clerk, Hudson, Joy, the telephonist, the enrichment of our standard of living, I've lost my prescription, Jane, my father's too old to be here, thank God, the National Research, Research Development Council, the Taylor Report, the Nayler Report, failure report, and a projected budget of five hundred thousand million, millions for this purpose, the practical dangers of pre-marital in the commanding heights of our declining objects.

JUDGE: Objects?

BILL: Objects? I think so, my lord. I think that's what I meant to be saying. (*Continuing.*) Facing up realistically, the issues that are important, really, central, social change, basic, burning issues.

JUDGE: I think that is evident.

BILL: I wish I could see more clearly.

JUDGE: Very well.
(*Pause.*)

CLERK: My lord, I have been retained by the defendant. However, after long discussion with myself, and my learned colleagues, he has expressed his

11

intention of conducting his own case.

JUDGE: I see. You have tried to dissuade him from this course?

CLERK: We have, my lord. He is quite adamant.

JUDGE: Mr. Maitland, you must be fully aware of the implication, of your decision?

BILL: Yes.

JUDGE: It is my duty to warn you of the difficulties that may be involved in discarding the services of learned counsel.

BILL: I see that. Except I wish I *could*.

JUDGE: And to warn you against taking an irrevocable decision which will almost certainly. . . .

BILL: But I'm incapable of making decisions.

JUDGE: Involve you in onerous difficulties, in view of the complexities we are faced with here. Even though, as a practising solicitor of, I believe, some standing and experience, you are no doubt better equipped to conduct yourself than would ordinarily be the case.

(BILL *smiles*.)

I put it to you now, once and for all; do you persist in this decision?

BILL: (*looks at* CLERK.) I do, my lord.

JUDGE: Very well.

(*Pause*.)

Proceed.

BILL: I beg your pardon?

JUDGE: Carry on, Mr. Maitland.

BILL: Me, my lord?

JUDGE: Yes. You, Mr. Maitland.

BILL: But what about them?

JUDGE: Are you—or are you not conducting your own case?

BILL: But them? What about them?

12

JUDGE: Mr. Jones, will, I believe, lead for the prosecution.

CLERK: That is correct, my lord.

JUDGE: Come then. Do let us get on.

BILL: He was supposed to be defending me.

JUDGE: Mr. Maitland. Have we not, just a few moments ago, established that you had dismissed Mr. Jones?

BILL: Yes.

JUDGE: And that you have elected to conduct your own defence?

BILL: Well, it is. I did. But then it shouldn't be me.

JUDGE: Shouldn't be you?

BILL: No.

JUDGE: What shouldn't be you?

BILL: Well, if it is. Why isn't he starting off then?

JUDGE: Starting off?

BILL: Yes.

(*Pause.*)

JUDGE: You have already started off.

(BILL *ponders.*)

BILL: But—I seem to have made some sort of absurd. . . . Isn't it? I mean: he should have started off first. In the very first place.

(*Pause.*)

JUDGE: That is true. However. . . . *You* have done so instead.

BILL: But what about the. . . .

JUDGE: That is my ruling. It is possible that it may be reversed or re-interpreted at another time elsewhere.

BILL: What about the last word?

JUDGE: I suggest you begin.

BILL: I shouldn't be the one to have to start off.

JUDGE: Possibly not, but you have, and the ruling is

13

quite clear.

BILL: (*bafflement. Tries to focus*). I ought to; have; the last word.

JUDGE: No doubt, we shall see in the event.

BILL: What event? I'm here, aren't I?

JUDGE: You must be aware, with your training and background, that the law can often be very flexible in these matters.

BILL: As your lordship pleases. As you say, it probably makes very little difference.

JUDGE: Demonstrably.

BILL: Before I—

JUDGE: Yes?

BILL: May I have a glass of water?

(*The* JUDGE *motions to the* CLERK, *who obliges.* BILL *tries to study his face.*)

My Lord—which one is Mr. Jones?

JUDGE: There. (*He indicates the* CLERK *a little impatiently*) (*The* CLERK *hands him the glass of water.*)

BILL: Please forgive me. I have rather a headache. Perhaps that's why I'm here now. I had too much to drink last night, that's just the simple truth of it. Well, when I say that, I mean not much more than I usually have. Most nights. But that's well, I do drink quite a lot. Quite a lot? Oh, anyway, I'm what you'd call a serious drinker. That's to say, I just don't mess about once I get going—when I do. When I do? I nearly always do. I can drink a whole bottle of whisky. Can't be any good for the heart, can it? It must be a strain, pumping all that fire and damned rigour and everything all out again? Still, I'm pretty strong. I must be. Otherwise, I couldn't take it. That is, if I *can* take it. I can't, I'm sorry, I can't find my pills.

14

I always have three or so in my ticket pocket.
So sorry.
(*Pause.*)
If you knew me, if you knew me, you'd know
I wouldn't come out without them. I'm so
sorry.
Just a moment. The glands or whatever these
lumps are in my neck feel as if they were trying
to batter their way out. Just here, trying to
force their way out. Like broken marbles, real
big gob stoppers. With chipped edges. I must
have left them in my overcoat pocket. Do you
think the constable could get my overcoat or
look in the left-hand pocket? Or the inside? It
shouldn't take a moment. Only. It's a bit like a
gimlet too. Right up behind the eyeballs. All
that and the marbles too.
(*Pause.*)
I know that none of this is very interesting to
you, but the fact is I could do a lot better, a
lot better, that is acquit myself, acquit myself
better. Yes. Well, they don't seem to be there,
my pills. Or tablets or whatever you call them.
What's the difference? Only: I really do need
three of them at least. And nothing else will do
the job properly. Then, if I keep my head
upright and don't move it about too much, and
talk fairly slowly, if you can bear with me, with
your lordship's indulgence, I can make a start.
Some sort of start, anway.

JUDGE: Do you think you can proceed now?

BILL: I have a feeling there is very little choice
involved. And so, I will do my best, your
lordship. I don't want you to think that
because of these minor difficulties—and—that

I have come here unprepared. I have always
expected this, and, consequently, I have done
my best to prepare myself as well as I can.

JUDGE: Yes?

BILL: In. With. Your lordship's indulgence, I will . . .
make some sort of a start.

JUDGE: Please.

BILL: And see what comes to me. In the event. Now:
I wish I could open my eyes. My eyelids.
They're like oysters. However, this is my
concern and not yours. I'll think of something.
(*He presses his eyeballs*). My name is William
Henry Maitland. I am thirty nine years old,
practising solicitor and commissioner for oaths
at 34, Fleet Chambers, E.C.3. I have worked in
service of the law—if you can call being a
solicitor, working in the service of the law—for
nearly twenty five years. In fact I started work
in this very office, this court, since I was at least
fifteen. Perhaps earlier. That—(*points to* JUDGE'*s
seat*)—is my old boss's chair. You see, I took
his position over from him. My managing clerk,
old Hudson, he was working for the old man
even then. Not that he was much older than me.
He just always seemed older. Anyway, he works
for me now. I don't even know why I took up
the law. I don't think there was any reason at
all much. I can't think of any now, and I
couldn't think of any then. Perhaps I did think
I might land up on the bench even. Or with
learned counsel. Mr. Jones. No, but I never
seriously thought of myself being brilliant
enough to sit in that company, with those men,
among any of them with their fresh complexions
from their playing fields and all that, with their

16

ringing, effortless voice production and their quiet chambers, and tailors and mess bills and Oxford Colleges and going to the opera God knows where and the 400, whatever I used to think that was. I can't remember at the time. I have always been tolerably bright.

JUDGE: Always been?

BILL: Bright. *Only* tolerably bright, my lord. But, to start with, and potentially and finally, that is to say, irredeemably mediocre. Even at fifteen, when I started out in my profession. Oh no, before that. Before that. Mark. I have never had any but fugitive reasons—recurrent for all that—that this simple, uncomplicated, well, simple, assumption was correct. I knew that in order to become even a small market place solicitor, as distinct even from a first rate managing clerk with a big, substantial firm, I should have to study very hard indeed for my, oh for my Law Society examinations all the while I was picking up probate and conveyancing, running out for jugs of tea, packets of fags for the other clerks or calling in the chemist for the telephonist.

JUDGE: Telephonist.

BILL: I'm afraid there's always one like that, my lord. Mine is called Joy. The one who works for me now, that is. This one was called Jill.

JUDGE: Is anything the matter?

BILL: I seem to have lost my drift, my lord. What's my wife doing here? Well, she would be here, of course. No, it's Sheila, it's my ex-wife. I didn't even know where she was. How did she know? They all seem to *find out* about these things. They find out. I'm sure my old man's

17

there, but I can't see him. I hope not. He'll hate this. I seem to have lost my drift, my lord.

JUDGE: (*kindly*) Mediocrity?

BILL: Well: it might perhaps be misleading to you and everyone to dwell on it too much. I merely wanted to draw your attention.

JUDGE: There is time enough, Mr. Maitland.

BILL: I have always had a certain facility, it's true. But little else. A fairly quick mind, not profound, a bit flashy I should say, indeed, *you* would say, not even that, a little more than perky. They said I had a quick mind, for getting fags and remembering things for a while, long enough to get my exams, for instance. A quick mind they said was useful, not that I had it, but helpful, as your lordship will know, in a profession where time doesn't mean a thing to anyone except some poor bloody agonized client who wants to know whether he's going to get the house he wants, an overdraft, or a divorce, eighteen months or a fine. However, however, my lord. I seem to retain very little. Very little indeed, hardly anything at all, in fact. Which is disturbing. Because I don't see how I can carry on my work even, well I am carrying on with it, but I must be getting less and less any good at it. *Even* my work, that's almost the least of it, which is probably, no doubt, one of the reasons I find myself here, in the dark dock arraigned before you. But both my clients and my colleagues seem to think, at least they used to think, I had a sort of dashing flair for making decisions, which might have been true to some extent. This can't hide the fact from me, and never has

18

done, that I am by nature indecisive. Nor will
it escape you, my lord. I am almost forty
years old, and I know I have never made a
decision which I didn't either regret, or suspect
was just plain commonplace or shifty or
scamped and indulgent or mildly stupid or
undistinguished. As you must see. As for why
I am here, I have to confess this: I have to
confess that: that I have depended almost
entirely on other people's efforts. Anything else
would have been impossible for me, and I
always knew in my own heart that only that it
was that kept me alive and functioning at all,
let alone making decisons or being quick
minded and all that nonsense about me. . . .
That I have never really been able to tell the
difference between a friend and an enemy, and I
have always made what seemed to me at the
time to make the most exhausting efforts to
find out. The difference. But it has never been
clear to me, and there it is, the distinction, and
as I have got older, and as I have worked my
way up—up—to my present position. I find
it even more, quite impossible. And out of the
question. And then, then I have always been
afraid of being found out.

JUDGE: Found out?

BILL: Yes.

JUDGE: Found out about what?

BILL: I'm sorry, my lord. I don't understand. I have
always been quite certain that this is where I
should end up, here, I've seen it too many
times, with you there and counsel over there.
There. And there. Down to the cells. Off to the
Scrubs, hand over your watch and your money,

19

take all your clothes off, have a bath, get examined, take all your clothes off in the cold, and the door shut behind you. I should like to stand down if I may. I am not feeling very well. I never hoped or wished for anything more than to have the good fortune of friendship and the excitement and comfort of love and the love of women in particular. I made a set at both of them in my own way. With the first with friendship, I hardly succeeded at all. Not really. No. Not at all. With the second, with love, I succeeded, I succeeded in inflicting, quite certainly inflicting, more pain than pleasure. I am not equal to any of it. But I can't escape it, I can't forget it. And I can't begin again. You see?

(*A torpid moan escapes him. Fade. The light remains on* BILL. *The* JUDGE *and the* CLERK *leisurely take off their wigs and robes, coming into the office area, hanging them on the upstage end of the coat stand. The* JUDGE *who is* HUDSON, *the* MANAGING CLERK, *speaks to the* CLERK *who is called* JONES. *During this,* BILL *remains still. The actor has to indicate the painful struggle into consciousness, without, at the same time, making the physical metaphor too explicit: the difficulty of breathing, the violent inner effort to throw off the burden, the fishy, palpitating struggle of the heart being landed into wakefulness. The gasping will takes over. The dream, the prison of embryonic helplessness for the moment, recedes, but not altogether. The focus fades on* BILL, *who emerges slowly out of it. Presently, he makes his way out of it, into the outer office, then through into the office*

20

itself.)

HUDSON: (*to* JONES.) Parky this morning.

JONES: Yes.

HUDSON: What's the matter then? Late night?

JONES: No, not specially.

HUDSON: How's that girl of yours?

JONES: O.K.

HUDSON: Still getting married?

JONES: Suppose so. Got to get these finals out of the way first. Hardly see her except on Sundays.
(SHIRLEY, *the secretary, comes in with post and hands it to* HUDSON.)

SHIRLEY: There's yours.

HUDSON: Thank you, Shirley. And how are you today?

SHIRLEY: Looking forward to Friday night, thank you.

JONES: Is mine there?

SHIRLEY: Why don't you try looking for it? (*Goes out.*)

HUDSON: What's up with her?

JONES: Dunno. Packing it in, she says.

HUDSON: What, again?

JONES: I think she means it this time.
(BILL *comes into* OUTER OFFICE *fairly briskly.*)

BILL: Morning all!

JONES: Better start getting it sorted out myself then.

BILL: (*coming in.*) Sorry I'm late.

HUDSON: You're the boss.

BILL: I couldn't get a taxi. That's the first time I've never got one. All got their bloody lights on and all going home. I don't know what they're doing.
(*Goes to desk. He has a plaster by his ear.*)

HUDSON: Cut yourself?

BILL: Yes.

HUDSON: I don't know why——

BILL: Why I don't use an electric razor. There's

21

quite enough almighty racket going on in the
world without tuning it into my chin the minute
I wake up.

HUDSON: But it's so simple.

BILL: Not for me it isn't. Two bathrooms in my
house and my wife has to use mine while I'm
having a quiet little shave to myself. She has to
talk.

HUDSON: Not your morning.

BILL: Can't be worse than the evening.

HUDSON: What, have a skinful, did you?

BILL: More than that, one way and another.
(SHIRLEY *brings in* BILL'*s post and puts it in front
of him.*)

BILL: Hullo, sexy. Is that all?

HUDSON: Don't worry—there's enough here.

BILL: What—no make up this morning?

SHIRLEY: You *do* remember Mrs. Garnsey's coming at
9.30?

BILL: Of course, I forgot you girls don't really wear
makeup nowadays, do you? All leaking
eyeshadow and red noses. Go and put on some
lipstick, dear. What's the matter? Isn't he
giving it to you?

SHIRLEY: Finished?

BILL: Don't tell me you're getting too much. I don't
believe it.

SHIRLEY Oh, knock it off.

BILL: Well, something's made you bad tempered this
morning, and I don't believe that languid pipe
cleaner of an accountant you're engaged to has
got *that* much lead in his pencil.

SHIRLEY: Do you ever think of anything else?

BILL: Not so much. Probably less than you do
though.

22

SHIRLEY: Me?

BILL: I just talk about it at great boring length mostly to boring, bad tempered, and silly girls. Without make-up.

SHIRLEY: You know what you can do! And quick.

BILL: (*to* HUDSON.) Do you hear that, Wally? Do you think I should let her talk to me like that?

HUDSON: I think she'd better get back to her work. I'll see you in a minute, Shirley.
(*She nods and goes out.*)

BILL: And put some lipstick on!

HUDSON: Thought she was going to let you have it there for a minute.

BILL: What's the matter with her?

HUDSON: Jones here says she's giving in her notice.

BILL: But she does that every other month.

JONES: I think she means it this time.

BILL: Oh, why?
(BILL'*s manner to* JONES *is slightly hostile, more polite than he is to most people.*)

JONES: Oh—Just says she's fed up with the place.

BILL: And?

JONES: Oh, well just that really.

BILL: What else?

HUDSON: Well, out with it.

JONES: Well, this is just what she said to me——

BILL: He'd make a great witness wouldn't he? I wouldn't like to see you in the box up against someone like old Winters.

JONES: (*dimly nettled*). She just said last night while we were locking up that she was sick of the sight of Mr. Maitland and couldn't even bear to be in the same room with him.

BILL: She said what!

HUDSON: (*to* JONES). It's all right, you needn't repeat it.

JONES: Well, you asked me what she said.

HUDSON: You know what these girls are. They get a bit, you know. And Shirley's an independent sort of a——

BILL: What a funny thing to say. Do you think she meant it?

JONES: Dunno. Wasn't listening properly.

BILL: (*irritated*). I'll talk to her later. When she's calmed down a bit. (*To* HUDSON). Remind me. (HUDSON *looks amused.*)
What are you smirking about? Oh? Keep it outside of the office and all that? Look, I haven't touched that girl for months, not for about six or seven months at least. *I've* done no harm to her. If she's unhappy it's not my fault. Besides, she's engaged.

HUDSON: That wouldn't stop you.

BILL: No, it wouldn't, but I didn't. It's probably that droopy young book-keeper making her miserable. Giving her dinner-dances on the Kingston By-Pass. The morning she came back from that she had red eyes for a week.

HUDSON: He seemed a nice, quiet, serious . . . fellow, I thought.

BILL: Nice, quiet, serious fellow, I thought. That just about sounds like every supine, cautious, young husband all about six degrees under proper consciousness in the land. The whole bloody island's blocked with those flatulent, purblind, mating weasels. You know who they are? Her fiancé? They're the ones who go out on Bank Holidays in the car! And have mascots in the rear window.

HUDSON: Well, it's their lives.

BILL: Yes, and if we only had enough Bank Holidays

24

they'd kill each other on every coast road from Blackpool to Brighton.

HUDSON: You're not suggesting they should all be killed off just because they don't please you?

BILL: I'm just suggesting we might hope they'll do it themselves for us.

HUDSON: You'll be getting one of your headaches in a minute.

BILL: Don't worry. I have. Do you know who they are?

HUDSON: No. Only don't forget Mrs. Garnsey.

BILL: Damn Mrs. Garnsey. She's probably one too. They: are the people who go up every year like it was holy communion to have a look at the Christmas decorations in Regent Street. They're the ones who drive the family fifty miles into the countryside and then park their cars beside the main road with a few dozen others, get out their thermos flasks, camp stools and primuses and do you know what they do? They sit and watch the long distance lorry drivers rattling past, and old people's coaches and all the other idiots like themselves about to do the same thing.

HUDSON: Sometimes I'd like to see you and old Winters have a go at each other—in court. I think you'd enjoy that.

BILL: Don't think I couldn't, either. He's not all that good. Just because he wears a wig and I don't.

HUDSON: Well, then——

BILL: This place'd be a lot different if you were running it, wouldn't it, Wally?

HUDSON: Everyone has their own methods. You've got yours.

BILL: Yes, but mine just aren't different. They're not respectable for a solicitor. But then I don't feel

25

like you do about the Law. I don't think the
law is respectable at all. It's there to be
exploited. Just as *it* exploits us.

HUDSON: You'll be putting young Jones here off the job.

BILL: I don't think there's much danger of that.

HUDSON: Well, we all have our different methods, as I
say. Different ways of looking at things.

BILL: Wally, do me a favour, will you? You'll be
be saying 'with all due respect', or 'be that as
it may' in a minute. I'd thought I'd broken you
of that stinking habit. No, I don't think young
Jones here is the type to end up goosing
telephonists and knocking off secretaries, to say
nothing of cooking up evidence on occasion or
risking collusive agreements. Do you have it off
with that girl of yours?

(JONES *is discomfited.*)

I'm sorry. That's an impertinent question. Isn't
it? Forget it.

JONES: Well——

BILL: No, don't bother. But I was right about what I
said?

JONES: Yes. Yes. I think so.

BILL: Why?

JONES: I just don't think it——

BILL: What?

JONES: Any of those things are really worth the
candle.

BILL: Not really worth the candle. No you're quite
right. It's not. Well, now we've disposed of the
candle, you'd better take it with you into
Shirley. She's probably in need of it. Have you
got plenty to do?

(JONES *nods.*)

Got to keep you busy. Busy, busy, busy. That's

26

what you want isn't it? That's why you came to me isn't it, for no other reason. See what's in, what business there is, any money in, any problems, anything else. Right?

JONES: Yes, Mr. Maitland. (*Goes.*)

HUDSON: What's the matter then?

BILL: What do you mean what's the matter then? (*Calls*) Shirley!

HUDSON: You seem to have it in a bit for him.

BILL: He's a tent peg. Made in England. To be knocked into the ground.
(SHIRLEY *appears.*)

SHIRLEY: Yes?

BILL: What? Oh, get me a glass of water, Shirley.

SHIRLEY: (*pause*). Helpless?
(*Goes out.* HUDSON *and* BILL *look at each other. More satisfaction for* HUDSON.)

HUDSON: I think you're wrong there. He's got quite a good brain. Bit slow for your taste, but you shouldn't underestimate him.

BILL: I don't. He's got all the makings of a good, happy, democratic underdog like that bitch's boyfriend who won't even get me a glass of water when I ask her. He irritates me. He doesn't like me any more than I like him. Why does he work for me?

HUDSON: Why don't you sack him?

BILL: What for? He does his work well enough. Doesn't he?

HUDSON: Fine.

BILL: Well then. Joy! He even laughs at my rotten jokes. Or anyway, his little filleted spine rattles about a bit. Otherwise—no sound. . . .
(JOY *appears.*)
Joy, get me a glass of water, will you?

27

JOY: O.K.

BILL: And ask Shirley—no, you'd better get it. See if you can bring in Mrs. Garnsey's file.

(*She goes out.*)

One thing I'll say for you, Wally, you've never pretended to laugh. Not even at my good ones.

HUDSON: We don't all have your sense of humour.

BILL: Well, don't sound so pleased about it. Anyway, I haven't got a sense of humour. I haven't had a good laugh for years. Not only that, Mr. Jones may find his finals and working for me won't do him a damn bit of good in the long run. Or you, for that matter.

HUDSON: What's that?

BILL: I say: soon we'll all be out of a job. If anyone's riddled with the idea that being busy is the same thing as being alive it's our young Jones.

HUDSON: What are you talking about?

BILL: Jones.

HUDSON: You're sure you're all right?

BILL: Sure, fine. Now what about Mrs. Garnsey, why are you shoving her on to me? No. I don't, I don't think I do. Things seem a bit odd. I still can't understand why I couldn't get a taxi. They all had their lights on: for hire.

HUDSON: Well, you know what they are.

BILL: Yes, but I've never known it to happen to me before. Not in the morning.

HUDSON: You look all right. But if you'd like to. . . .

BILL: And the caretaker turned his back on me. I was walking up the stairs and I was going to ask him—you know, quite politely—why the lift wasn't working. And he turned his back on me.

HUDSON: Didn't notice you, I expect.

BILL: No, he looked straight at me. And turned his

back on me.

HUDSON: Well, he's a contrary old devil.

BILL: Not with me, he hasn't been.

HUDSON: I gave him a quid at Christmas, and he didn't even give me a thank you.

BILL: I gave him five. (*Self-conscious*). Well, I know it's too much, but we had a drink together over at the 'Feathers'.

HUDSON: Too much is right.

(*Slight pause.*)

BILL: They won't need us much longer. They'll need no more lawyers. Have you seen the papers this morning? Some mathematical clerk will feed all our petitions and depositions and statements and evidence into some clattering brute of a computer and the answer will come out guilty or not guilty in as much time as it takes to say it. There'll be no more laws' delays, just the insolence of somebody's office. They'll need no more lawyers. I don't understand who will be needed.

HUDSON: I shouldn't think it'll quite come to that.

BILL: How do you know what we'll come to? Or when? Sometimes I wish I were older so I had less chance of finding out. (*Bangs newspaper.*) Look at this dozy bastard: Britain's position in the world. Screw that. What about my position? Vote wheedling catchfart, just waiting to get us into his bag and turn us out into a lot of little technological dogs turning his wheel spit of endless bloody consumption and production. Why doesn't he stick his scientific rod—into the Red Sea or where he likes and take everyone he likes with him—including Jones. The sooner the sea closes up behind them the better. With

29

Jones entering the Promised Land in his mini.

HUDSON: Oh, leave the boy alone. What's he done to you. Anyway, he's got a motor bike.

BILL: Even better. I can't think of a better way to emerge—in an emergent country. Why don't they all go and emerge? Emerge.

HUDSON: Why don't *you* do a bit of emerging yourself?

BILL: I'm never likely to do that.

(*Pause.*)

HUDSON: Well, we should make a start. (*Joke*). Before they move in the computers.

(BILL *doesn't respond.*)

BILL: Joy! What are you doing?

JOY: (*off*). Coming.

HUDSON: Seen that Betty lately?

BILL: Where's my glass of water? Which Betty?

HUDSON: Oh, were there more?

BILL: I know three girls called Betty. No. Four.

HUDSON: What a life. I don't know.

BILL: She married some corpulent financier.

HUDSON: Who?

BILL: Betty.

(JOY *comes in with glass of water and a file.*)
I'm always seeing his name on building sites. Spends his time pulling down Regency squares —you know—and putting up slabs of concrete technological nougat. Like old, pumped up air-raid shelters. Or municipal lavatories. She's a nice kid. Don't see much of her now. Seen her at some of those theatre first nights he's so fond of. Hemmed in by all his thrusting sycophants —I think she can hardly see him through her mink. Jones now.

JOY: Sorry. Shirley wouldn't tell me where to find it.

BILL: Jones should work for him. Britain's future.

30

Betty's old man is certainly one of the
architects. What's that, my love?

JOY: Your glass of water.

BILL: Oh, thank you. At last, a friend.

JOY: Mrs. Garnsey's file. Shirley——

BILL: Yes, I'm sure. And how are you?

JOY: I'm all right thank you. Is that all?

BILL: Not enough for me. She looks pretty today,
don't you think, Wally.

HUDSON: Yes. She does.

BILL: When are we going to have an orgy together?

JOY: You can't have an orgy with two.

BILL: No, but you can make a start.
(*She smiles and goes out.*)
Look at that beautiful bottom. Don't go much
on her face. But the way her skirt stretches over
that little bum. You could stick a bus ticket in
there. Joy. What do you think, Wally?

HUDSON: Yes, it's quite nice, I suppose.

BILL: It's a beauty. Wonder what's she like?

HUDSON: No doubt you'll find out.

BILL: Don't know. Maybe not. Like who was it.
You know, Dr. Johnson said whatsit, 'Paradise
Lost': more of a beauty than a pleasure. Still
she looks as though she could do with a bit.
She's got the galloping cutes all right. Joy.
She's had more joy sticks than hot dinners.

HUDSON: I was only waiting for that. What about Mrs.
Garnsey?

BILL: I have an extraordinary thing about blondes.
They're like plague carriers for me. Even dyed
blondes. My first wife was blonde. *Really*
blonde. Blonde, blonde, *blonde!* It was *beautiful.*
I've never known hair nicer. Right: Mrs.
Garnsey.

31

HUDSON: Well, try and let her settle down a bit, will you?
Joy, I mean. She's only just mastered that
simple little switchboard. If *you* get started on
her, we'll get nowhere.

BILL: Right. No Joy. For the moment, anyway. Goes
against the Rules. Which is the best thing.
Right: work, work. Mrs. Garnsey. Where are
my pills? There should be some in here.
Anyway, I always keep three in reserve in my
ticket pocket. Where the hell are they? Joy!
Wish I didn't drink so much. And I keep
wanting to sleep. I finally took a pill at four
this morning, went off at five, then I couldn't
get up. I couldn't even move at first.
(JOY *appears.*)
I was all trussed up. My darling, have you seen
my pills, my headache pills?

JOY: No, sorry.

BILL: Never mind, here they are. I might just do a bit
better with Mrs. Garnsey when she comes. Ask
her to wait five minutes when she comes. Give
her a cup of that stinking tea you and young
Jones brew up together.

JOY: O.K. (*Goes out.*)

BILL: I don't know whether I really like that blonde
bat or not. She's rather a tuneful little thing, if
you know what I mean. Wally, try not to let
me have anything to drink at lunch-time.
O.K.?

HUDSON: I'll do my best.

BILL: 'And if I drink oblivion of a day, so shorten I
the stature of my soul.' Who said that now?
Some poor crazy bastard—Blake I think. Just
bitter lemon, all right?

HUDSON: Right.

(JOY *re-appears.*)

JOY: Oh, and your wife rang just before you got in.
I said you'd ring back.

BILL: Right, thanks.

JOY: Shall I get her for you?

BILL: No, not just for the moment. But remind me.
(*She goes out.*)
She knows how long it takes me to get here.

HUDSON: But you couldn't get a taxi. Remember?

BILL: I've always managed to keep everything in
place, in place enough to get on with it, do my
work, enjoy things, enjoy other people, take
an interest in all kinds of things. I've tried to
read, not just my own subject. I keep trying and
the circle just seems to get smaller. If Anna
rings will you speak to her, say I'm with Mrs.
Garnsey?
(HUDSON *nods.*)
It's only about next weekend.

HUDSON: I thought you were going to Blackpool. On a
business trip.

BILL: Yes, with Liz. We'd planned it before
Christmas. We haven't really had a long
weekend together since last summer when
Anna took the kids with her down to North
Devon.

HUDSON: So what's happening?

BILL: I don't know. Anna's fixed some crazy do for
the entire weekend for the girl's birthday.

HUDSON: How old is she?

BILL: I don't know. Seventeen. Eighteen. Anyway, too
old and too sophisticated and too unhampered
by anything in particular to need my presence
at her birthday for two whole days.

HUDSON: Does your wife know about Blackpool?

33

BILL: Cancel it, she says. Business doesn't mean all that to *you*. Give your daughter a good time.

HUDSON: She knows you were going with Liz?

BILL: Why else should she arrange this daft junket? She doesn't like the kids' chums any more than I do. It'll be all jazz and noise and black leather and sour teenage squalor and necking, and oh—

HUDSON: You've always been pretty fond of necking and——

BILL: Squalor! I may have helped to knock it together often enough but I haven't enjoyed it, and I haven't ever been made to feel sharp or with it or representative of any damned thing. I was never, at any time, like that bunch of kids my daughter runs around with, so don't compare me to them.

HUDSON: Sorry.

BILL: And as for necking, I never went in for it, never would, and pray God I am never so old, servile or fumbling that I ever have to wriggle through that dingy assault course. Do you like it, do you want it, those are the only questions I have ever thought worth while going into. You think I'm not telling the truth? Well, it's as near the truth as I can find at this moment; for one thing I have never had very strong fingers which is why I had to give up learning the piano.

HUDSON: What are you going to do then?

BILL: Do?

HUDSON: About the weekend?

BILL: I've no idea. I don't know which is worse, which prospect frightens me more. I keep seeing their faces. Anna's. Liz. And some of the others. It's even worse when they ring up. Not that

34

Liz rings very often. She has an immaculate
idea of a mistress's rights. I want to feel tender,
I want to be comforting and encouraging and
full of fun and future things and things like
that. But all I feel is as if my head were bigger
and bigger, spiked and falling off, like a mace,
it gets in my way, or keeps getting too close.
It's not worth the candle is it?

HUDSON: Certainly doesn't seem like it, does it?

BILL: No. But then I've never discovered what is.
That blessed candle of yours and Jones, the
Holy Grail of the people who hold back.

HUDSON: No, it's just that some people seem to use
things like sex, for instance, as a, a place of, of
escape, instead of objects, well—in themselves.

BILL: Yes, I know what you mean. I've thought of
that. But what about work? I know we're not
doing any at the moment, but we're going to,
we both work pretty hard, Wally. *You*
certainly do, and you don't get a great deal for
it. And I think even you'll admit I work harder
than most when I'm actually at it.

HUDSON: Oh, sure.

BILL: But what sort of object is that? Is it an
enjoyment, a duty, an obligation, a necessity
or just the effort of fighting, of fighting off the
end, whatever is to come to you.

HUDSON: I don't know. I don't think it matters all that
much. So long as you're reasonably interested
in what you do. You mustn't ask for too much.

BILL: Then you don't get disappointed. Mrs.
Garnsey'll be disappointed if we don't get her
her divorce all right. You're quite right, Wally,
as usual. Anyway, why have you foisted Mrs.
Garnsey on to me? I thought you and Jones

35

had been dealing with her up till now. There's nothing specially difficult is there?

HUDSON: No, nothing special.

BILL: Well?

HUDSON: We've both got rather a lot on at the moment.

BILL: Well, so have I. I'm supposed to be at the Scrubs by 11.30 to see that Bennet kid.

HUDSON: What that? The indecent assault?

BILL: Yes. We didn't get very far. He was too upset. Clothes off, possessions signed for, bath, medical inspection in the whistling cold, keys jangling. He wasn't in any state for anything. I don't know why we do any criminal work.

HUDSON: I couldn't agree more.

BILL: I thought if I did Mrs. Garnsey, you'd go down to see Bennet. I suppose it's not your line?

HUDSON: Not really.

BILL: But does it depress you?

HUDSON: No. I just don't go for it, you might say.

BILL: You'd rather not do divorce either.

HUDSON: I don't feel that strongly. I get a bit fed up listening to it, trying to find out what really did happen all the time. But I don't actually mind it. I just wouldn't go out of my way to choose it, that's all.

BILL: What would you choose? Straight-forward bit of complicated conveyancing.

HUDSON: I'd say divorce was *your* line. Living other people's lives.

BILL: What do you mean by that?

HUDSON: I thought you enjoyed it.

BILL: Enjoyed what?

HUDSON: Oh, you know. Probing, taking a part.

BILL: You mean I'm not detached enough.

HUDSON: No, I didn't say that.

BILL: I don't want to live anyone's life, not anyone's. I dread those clients, clients like Mrs. Garnsey. I've got all the lumber I can carry. Are you sure you can't get along to see Bennet?

HUDSON: Don't see how I can.

BILL: Does he disgust you that much?

HUDSON: Nothing disgusts me. Any longer. I am simply not very interested or aroused by contemplating such people or such things. Apart from that, I've got to take Mrs. Rose down to counsel at eleven. That'll take till lunch time for certain. I've tried to piece it all together, but she never says the same thing twice in the same breath.

BILL: What is it? She lying about her husband?

HUDSON: Oh yes, I think so.

BILL: What's he supposed to have done?

HUDSON: Kicked her up the bottom with his heavy gardening boots on, locked her out of the house all night, and she had to sleep in the car in her nightdress.

BILL: What else?

HUDSON: Not much. Something about hot table spoons. But nothing really admissible.

BILL: Was it a cold night?

HUDSON: What? Oh, in the car. Right in the middle of the big freeze-up. She says she got 'flu as a result and nearly got pneumonia.

BILL: Nearly?

HUDSON: And pleurisy.

BILL: Nearly. Why didn't she go for a drive with the heater on?

HUDSON: What, in her nightie at two o'clock in the morning?

BILL: Sounds a very romantic thing to do to me. She

37

could have taken a turn up the Great West
Road in her old man's car and ended up at
some pull-in with a bacon sandwich and a cup
of tea. I should think she'd have been made
very welcome.

HUDSON: Well, her husband had the keys of the car.
(*Pause.*)
I can see you don't like her.

BILL: Me? Haven't met her have I? I'm just
listening to you.

HUDSON: No. But I don't think you'd go much on her.
That's why I've done it.

BILL: Good old Wally. She'll get a good run out of
you. And you'll get your revenge watching her
withering in front of Winters. I—as you'd
expect—feel sorry for her husband. Old heavy
garden boots. What's he sound like?

HUDSON: Difficult to say. Excessive sexual demands. All
that.

BILL: Oh yes. King Kong, according to her, I suppose.

HUDSON: Perversions.

BILL: Spectacular?

HUDSON: Oh, usual sort of thing.

BILL: And what's she got? A wall eye and varicose
veins, I'll bet. He sounds fairly ordinary.

HUDSON: No, I don't think he's such a bad chap. Still—

BILL: Any adultery?

HUDSON: She says so, but there doesn't seem to be much
evidence. Winters has seen the papers. He didn't
seem to think much of it. I'm afraid he won't
touch it under 300. Still, if he can get her to
stick to her story, we should get him on cruelty.

BILL: You've applied for alimony and maintenance?

HUDSON: You bet.

BILL: Poor bastard. Well, what about Jones?

38

HUDSON: What about him?

BILL: Well, couldn't he go along to the Scrubs for me?

HUDSON: I suppose he could. If you really want him to.

BILL: No. You're right. I'd best do that myself. I don't think Jones would exactly inspire poor old Bennet with the confidence to go through with his appeal at all.

HUDSON: Anyway, I think he's pretty busy this morning.

BILL: Perhaps I should ring Anna now—and get it over before Mrs. Garnsey. Get it *over*—what am I thinking of?

HUDSON: He's got that Pole in again this morning. Third time in a week.

BILL: Pole?

HUDSON: You know—Zubuski, or whatever his name is.

BILL: Joy, get me Mrs. Maitland will you? What's up with him?

HUDSON: Well, he wants a divorce.

BILL: Grounds?

HUDSON: Adultery.

BILL: Well?

HUDSON: Well, the thing is this, sufficient evidence all right, I don't think there's any doubt of that, but he wants it on his own terms.

BILL: What do you mean: his own terms?

HUDSON: Quite simple. He insists on having sexual relations with his wife three times a week until the case comes up.

BILL: And the wife?

HUDSON: Oh, she agrees.

BILL: Well—good for them. (*Laughs.*)

HUDSON: Extraordinary, isn't it?

BILL: Yes.

HUDSON: We've both tried speaking to him. He just gets

furious and won't listen.

BILL: What's he going to do? Report us to the Law Society? What's really extraordinary is you and Jones.

HUDSON: Well, I suppose it's funny.

BILL: Yes. I think it is.

(*His laugh is interrupted by buzz and* JOY's *voice from his desk.*)

JOY: Mrs. Eaves is on the line.

BILL: (*pause*). I'll —no, tell her I'll ring her back as soon as I can.

HUDSON: (*pleased*). Well, there's number two bringing up the rear already. Busy morning.

BILL: Come on. Be fair. It isn't often Liz rings up. Not like Anna now.

HUDSON: Well, there is——

BILL: I know: Anna's my wife. There's never any doubt which side you're on.

HUDSON: I'm not on any side.

BILL: Yes you are. Wives and angels. Me: mistresses and devils. No. I'm not the one who's on any side. I don't have any idea of where I am. I have tried not to cause pain, I really have, you think I haven't, but I do try, I ought to be able to give a better account of myself. But I don't seem to be functioning properly. I don't seem to retain anything, at least not for very long. I wish I could go back to the beginning, except I wouldn't do any better. They used to say I had a quick brain.

HUDSON: Well, you have that.

BILL: No, I haven't. I have a very small, sluggish, slow moving brain. I just run it through quickly, at the wrong speed like a piece of film, and it darts and flickers, but it perceives little,

40

and it retains nothing. What do you think I
should do, Wally?

HUDSON: About the weekend? Tell Liz the truth.
(*Pause.*)

BILL: I'm always trying to do that. I'd like to cheer
her up for once, to go in free and uncluttered
and tell her we'd got three whole days together.

HUDSON: Well, do that then.

BILL: Thanks for the advice. I can see what put you
in this business. What's your problem, Mrs.
Garnsey? Well, legally you can do this. Or that.
I would advise this. However, you may prefer
to do that. Morally—or emotionally—do as
you like.

HUDSON: I don't know.

BILL: What? How she puts up with me.
(HUDSON *nods.*)

BILL: Which? Anna or Liz?

HUDSON: Either of them.

BILL: But especially Anna.

HUDSON: There must be some compensations. You've got
two nice kids.

BILL: They're all right. I don't think they think we're
as nice as we assume *they* are. Do you know
that boy actually *wanted* to go away to boarding
school. I told him he was crazy. But he
couldn't wait. Couldn't *wait*. And he writes dull
beady little letters all about house matches
and photographic societies and getting up at
God knows what hour every morning to go
swimming—in February. It's like having a
priest in the family.

HUDSON: How old is he?

BILL: Eleven! At his age I was thinking about girls.
Madeleine Caroll.

41

HUDSON: (*doing his irony*). Perhaps he's just a late
　　　　　developer.

　BILL: Seems to me he's in the right place to stay that
　　　　 way.

HUDSON: Still, he's happy.

　BILL: Blissful. I don't understand. I think I'd rather
　　　　 be in the Scrubs. Same thing really. Chaplains,
　　　　 lousy food, hard work, lights out, no birds.

HUDSON: Well, he's growing up.

　BILL: Yes. That's what Anna says. Perhaps she should
　　　　 have married *you*. You have so many points of
　　　　 agreement.

HUDSON: I'm all right, thank you.

　BILL: Yes. You are. But I don't think Anna is quite
　　　　 as absorbed in her children as yours. I mean,
　　　　 she hasn't turned their growing up into some
　　　　 protracted act of holy communion that'll end
　　　　 up with an empty chalice and hot flushes when
　　　　 she's fifty.
　　　　 (HUDSON *looks uncomfortable*.)
　　　　 (*Pause.*)
　　　　 I've asked you this before: do you think I
　　　　 should leave her?

HUDSON: I've told you before. I don't think it makes any
　　　　　difference. To you.
　　　　 (JOY'*s voice from desk*.)

　JOY: Your wife, Mr. Maitland.

　BILL: Right. (*Motions to* HUDSON *to stay*.) Shan't be a
　　　　 minute. (*On phone*.) Hullo. Hullo, love. Sorry,
　　　　 I was late. I couldn't get a cab. It was strange.
　　　　 Yes. First time I've never managed it. Even the
　　　　 old famous whistle didn't work. . . . Do I? . . .
　　　　 No, I don't think so. . . . Only old Wally.
　　　　 Trying to get sorted out. . . . Well, my
　　　　 darling, I'm sorry if I do happen to sound like

that. I didn't sleep as you know, or not much,
and. . . well, perhaps I am feeling a bit odd and
you can just hear it that's all. I've got a client
coming in any minute. . . .

(WALLY *goes out in spite of* BILL'*s signals.*)

No, of course, it's all right. That's why I rang
you back. I just haven't got started, and nothing
seems to be working very well. . . . What's that?
Yes. . . . Well, I know. Well. I'm sorry. . . . I
wish I could. What's that?. . . . I don't seem to
be able to hear. . . . I said I'm sorry. It's a
rotten line. . . . I can't *hear* you very well. . . .
Yes, that's a bit better. . . . Look, why don't I
ring you back, . . . what about lunch time. . . .
No, I can't have lunch. . . . Well, I've got to go
down to the Scrubs. . . . Well, I can't get
anyone else to go, then I'm seeing counsel, and
I'm in court the rest of the day, then I'm. . . .
Yes, Bennet. . . . Well, I think I'm the best
judge of that. . . . Well, a lot of people would
agree with you, especially on the bench. . . .
I'll probably be late. . . . I'm not sure yet. . . .
You know it's no good asking me at this time
of day. . . . Eight or nine. I don't know. It
might even be later. . . . If that's what you
think . . . well, if that's what you know, why
bother to ask me the question. . . . Look, please
don't, why don't I ring you? I may get away,
we'll see. . . . You know I haven't decided. . . .
That's how I cut myself—at half past eight,
remember. . . . I've told you: I don't know
yet. . . . I simply don't know. . . . I don't know
now, all I know is I probably am. . . . Well, it
won't be the greatest disappointment of her life
as you well know and I know, and *she* knows.

Look, love, I've got Wally waiting to go down to Winters. . . . Why don't you go out and . . . all right . . . well, I'm sorry you're feeling like that . . . oh, headache, . . . yes, the usual only a bit worse . . . and just odd things . . . well . . . all right . . . look after yourself. . . . I'm sorry, love. . . . I promised not to say that any more. . . .

(*He puts the 'phone down. Stares. Looks at the file in front of him. Drinks some more water. Presses eyeballs.*)

JOY: (*voice*).When do you want me to get Mrs. Eaves?

BILL: When I ask you to. No. Er, remind me will you, love? Perhaps after Mrs. Garnsey. . . .

JOY: She's not turned up yet.

BILL: Well, ask Mr. Hudson if he'll come back in, will you? And—get me another glass of water.

JOY: O.K. Oh. And I think Shirley wants to see you when you've a minute.

BILL: All right, when I've time. How's your sex life out there?

JOY: Thrilling. How's yours?

BILL: Oh—fairly quiet. Come in and see me.

JOY: When?

BILL: Oh—before you leave work.

JOY: O.K.

BILL: And—oh, I've asked you, haven't I?

JOY: Have you?

BILL: I don't know.

(HUDSON *appears.* JOY *switches out.*)

HUDSON: D'you want me?

BILL: Yes. Yes, was there anything else?

HUDSON: No, no I don't think so.

BILL: Nothing to sign?

44

HUDSON: No.

BILL: Right.

HUDSON: Well, I'd——

BILL: You'd better get on.

(HUDSON *turns to go*.)

Wally, Wally, there's just one thing I'd like to bring up.

HUDSON: Will it take long?

BILL: No, but I'd like to have a chat about it. Why? Aren't you interested or something?

HUDSON: I've just got rather—

BILL: O.K. O.K.

HUDSON: And I think Shirley's a bit keen to see you.

BILL: Shirley? Yes, I just thought this seemed like a good time to bring it up.

(*Pause*.)

HUDSON: Well, I'll drop in later then.

(SHIRLEY *comes in with glass of water*.)

BILL: Wally! Wally, try and pop in before you go down to Winters. I'll try and get through Mrs. Garnsey quickly. After all, Jones can take a lot of the stuff down from her. . . .

HUDSON: Just as you like. (*Goes out*).

(BILL *looks more than deserted. He looks at* SHIRLEY *gratefully. She hands him the water*.)

BILL: Thank you love, that's very kind of you.

(*He drinks. She watches*.)

Anything the matter?

SHIRLEY: Not with me there isn't.

BILL: Sure? You all right?

SHIRLEY: Fine, thank you.

BILL: Then what is it? We're friends aren't we? Why are you like this?

SHIRLEY: I'm not like anything.

BILL: Then?

45

SHIRLEY: I just want you to know I'm giving in my notice, that's all. You owe me a week's holiday but I'll give you a week, anyway.

BILL: But what for?

SHIRLEY: I've just made up my mind I'm going, that's all. Do you mind?

BILL: Of course I mind——

SHIRLEY: Well, that's bad luck for you, isn't it?

BILL: I don't know, love. Perhaps it's bad luck for both of us.

SHIRLEY: Not for me it isn't. I don't why I didn't clear out before.

BILL: You've always gone on about it——

SHIRLEY: And who talked me out of it?

BILL: What have I done?

SHIRLEY: Nothing. I'm just giving you notice. O.K.?

BILL: But—you must have a reason.

SHIRLEY: Sure, I've got reasons. Do I have to tell them to you?

BILL: No.

SHIRLEY: I've had enough.

BILL: What of?

SHIRLEY: Do you think I mean you?

BILL: I don't know. I don't know. I honestly don't know. If you wouldn't be in such a rush, perhaps I could——

SHIRLEY: Oh, well if you must know what for, for one thing, I'm pregnant.

BILL: You're what?

SHIRLEY: Mit child, dear. You'd had two haven't you? At least.

BILL: I'm sorry. (*Trying to focus*). I thought you were on the pills.

SHIRLEY: I was. I got fed up with them.

BILL: But you've only just got engaged.

46

SHIRLEY: So?

BILL: You mean you're going to get married?

SHIRLEY: That had always been the idea.

BILL: And you still want to?

SHIRLEY: Do I have to ask for your blessing or something?

BILL: I'm just a bit taken aback.

SHIRLEY: These things do happen, you know.

BILL: Are you really in love with him?

SHIRLEY: I thought you didn't go much on being in love.

BILL: Does he know?

SHIRLEY: I told him last night.

BILL: (*irritated*). Well?

SHIRLEY: He said he'd rather have waited a bit, he's quite pleased. What's the matter? Seen something?

BILL: Naturally, I see you a little differently. . . . I mean physically. . . . I feel. . . .

SHIRLEY: Poor you! You should feel like I do.

BILL: Is this the right thing?

SHIRLEY: Why? Should I ask advice from you? Father?

BILL: No, Shirley, no, don't do all that, I'm concerned——

SHIRLEY: Look—you can stick your long farewell. I just want you to know now: I'm pregnant.
(*Even* SHIRLEY'*s flush of relish is abated by* BILL'*s dismay. Pause. Quieter.*)
I'm getting married. And I'm giving in my notice. A week Friday. O.K.?

BILL: O.K., love
(*She waits.*)
When is it?

SHIRLEY: Fortnight.

BILL: No. The baby.

SHIRLEY: Oh. September.

47

BILL: September! But that's, that's about nine months
away.

SHIRLEY: Seven.

BILL: You could go on working for ages yet.
Everybody does.

SHIRLEY: Well, *I've* decided not to.

BILL: What about the money? You'll need that more
than ever now.

SHIRLEY: We'll manage.

BILL: But think how useful it'd be. What'll you do all
day, sitting round the house, waiting like some
silly bomb to go off?

SHIRLEY: Ted's doing all right.

BILL: But with two of you working—you'll need all
sorts of things——

SHIRLEY: He doesn't want me to go on.

BILL: He doesn't want me to go on! Who is he?
Godfrey Winn? He'll do what you *want*. Do
you want more money? You know you can
have it. Of course you can. You're worth it.
You're worth it to anybody.

SHIRLEY: Perhaps I might go to anybody.

BILL: No, stay here. You're wanted here.

SHIRLEY: What's all this, are you bribing everyone now?

BILL: Shirley, I'm very fond of you. What you've
told me——

SHIRLEY: Don't tell me you're short of it.

BILL: No, I'm *not*!

SHIRLEY: Anyway, that's out.

BILL: I haven't touched you——

SHIRLEY: Oh. (*Pause.*) Forget it.

BILL: I haven't touched you. You're accusing me. But
I haven't touched you. Not for three months.
At least.

SHIRLEY: Thanks so much.

48

BILL: Oh, for God's sake, throw off that half baked, cheap, show-girl act and listen to me.

SHIRLEY: Why? What have you ever done for me?

BILL: Nothing. I suppose. But I do know we had some affection for one another, beneath all the arguing and banter and waste of breath. I know I liked you. And when we were in bed together you dropped all your pretences and deceits, after a while anyway. Perhaps I did even. I don't think I let you think it was an enduring love affair—in the sense of well of endless, wheedling obligations and summonses and things. But, if you think back on it, detail by detail, I don't think you can say it was fraudulent. Can you?

SHIRLEY: No.

BILL: You can't *disown* it. If you do that, you are helping, you are conspiring to kill me. (*Pause.*)

SHIRLEY: One weekend in Leicester on client's business. Two weekends in Southend on client's business. Moss Mansions—remember them? Four days in Hamburg on client's business. One crummy client's crummy flat in Chiswick. And three times on *this* floor.(*She moves to go*). And another thing, just don't push any more of Joy's work on to me. I don't intend doing it. Any more than I like you, any more than I like your promising me for your clients when you're too busy with your wife or that Mrs Eaves or— I think you'd better forget about my notice. I'm going now. (*She goes out.*)
(*Presently* JOY *buzzes.*)

JOY: (*voice.*) Mrs. Garnsey is downstairs. (*Pause.*)

I said Mrs Garnsey is downstairs.

BILL: (*croaks.*) Would you? Ask her to wait! Could you, could you send in Mr. Hudson?

JOY: He's just on his way out.

BILL: Well, stop him.

JOY: I think he's gone.

BILL: I need him. Get him.

JOY: Well, I'll do my best.

BILL: And then I want to speak to Mrs Eaves.
(*Silence.* BILL *tries to look through Mrs. Garnsey's file.* HUDSON *enters, wearing his overcoat.*)

HUDSON: You want me?

BILL: Oh, yes. Wally.

HUDSON: Only I'm just off. You know what old Winters is like. Can't keep him waiting two minutes.

BILL: Won't take a minute.
(HUDSON *looks at his watch.*)
What would you say to becoming a partner?
(*Pause.*)
Eh?
(HUDSON *seems to react rather pleasurably.*)

HUDSON: I don't know. Really.

BILL: Well?

HUDSON: Are you asking me?

BILL: Yes. Yes. I am.

HUDSON: I see. Well. . . .

BILL: I realise it's a bit. . . .

HUDSON: Yes. Well. Needs a bit of thinking about, doesn't it?

BILL: Sure. Sure. Why don't we talk about it later? Chew it over.

HUDSON: Yes. Right. O.K. I will. Well thanks then. I'd. . . .

50

BILL: You're not thinking of leaving?

HUDSON: No. Not exactly.

BILL: You mean you *are* thinking of leaving?

HUDSON: I wouldn't say that exactly.

BILL: What would you say exactly?

HUDSON: I have had an offer, as a matter of fact.

BILL: Who from?

HUDSON: Several actually.

BILL: Who?

HUDSON: Well. . . .

BILL: Oh come on Wally, for God's sake.

HUDSON: Well, Piffards——

BILL: Piffards! Those crooks!

HUDSON: Very high class crooks. *If* that's what you think
they are.

BILL: Well, as you know, I think they're crooks, so
do you really. Still, if you want to wear striped
trousers and work for Cabinet Ministers'
wives.

(*Pause.*)

As you would say, we all have our ways of
looking at these things. O.K., then. Well,
perhaps you'll have a think about it?

HUDSON: (*smiles, then slowly.*) Yes. I will. Better get Mrs.
Rose down to the inquisition then. Cheerio.
(*Goes out.*)

BILL: Joy. Did you get my call to Mrs. Eaves!

JOY: She's engaged.

BILL: Well, keep trying. Tell the exchange to break in.
Where's Shirley?

JOY: She's gone.

BILL: Gone where?

JOY: I don't know.

BILL: I mean do you think she's coming back?

JOY: No idea. Shouldn't think so somehow.

51

BILL: Really?

JOY: She took her soap and towel.

BILL: What'd she say?

JOY: She was just crying. Shall I send in Mrs. Garnsey?

BILL: No. I must speak to Mrs. Eaves.

JOY: Oh, wait a minute, I think they've got it. Hold on. . . . You're through.

BILL: (*on phone.*) Liz? My darling, I've been trying to get hold of you. . . . Are you all right? . . . Well, no. . . . Everything's . . . I said everything's. . . . What? Oh, I couldn't get a taxi for a start, well, not a start. . . . Well, you know, if I keep my head upright and don't move it about too much, and talk fairly slowly. . . . Look, try and bear with me a minute. . . . What was what like? Oh, last night. . . . Well, yes there was an Anna situation . . . oh, before we went out and afterwards. . . . Yes, that was bad enough, but the whole thing was very strange. . . . It's difficult to explain. . . . No, I can't quite. . . . I'm sorry. I just don't seem to retain very much of anything, of anything that happened. . . . I just felt everyone was cutting me. . . cutting me . . . I know, I should care! I like them as much as they like me. . . . I don't know whether they're more afraid than I am. . . . I think they really *want* to be liked . . . in that sort of way. . . . I don't exactly do my best do I. No, well then. . . . No, Anna quite enjoyed herself while she was there. . . . Oh, the usual shower. . . . They all seem to adore her . . . I know, but more than ever . . . it's only all right when I'm with her. . . . Yes. . . . But it seemed at my expense this time, it seemed to be out of me . . .

52

as if they were disowning me . . . it's wonderful
to hear your voice. . . . Well, I don't know yet
. . . sometime this evening. . . . Look, please
don't *you* press me. . . . Yes. It'll be all right.
. . . I may not sound like it, but it will be. . .
you don't think I want to go to her silly
birthday junket, do you? . . . Do you think I
don't know that? Of course it's Anna. . . .
Well, I'll probably talk to the kid myself. . . .
Look, love, I've got to go. . . . Can I ring you
back? I've got this client and she's been waiting
about. . . . Let me ring you. . . . You *will* be in,
won't you? . . . Yes, but you will *be* there. . . .
Promise? Don't go out till I ring you back. . . .
I need to talk to you. . . . It'll be all right.
Don't worry. (*to* JOY.) I'll see Mrs. Garnsey
now.

(JOY *shows* MRS. GARNSEY *in.* BILL *rises to greet
her.*

Mrs. Garnsey, I'm so sorry I've kept you
waiting.

(MRS. GARNSEY *nods.*)

Have you had a cup of tea? Joy?

(JOY *nods. Goes out.*)

Right. I had a client on. I'm afraid I couldn't
get her off. Now: you've already had several
little sessions with Mr. Hudson haven't you?

MRS. GARNSEY: That's right.

BILL: Yes. Well, I haven't been into it in great detail.
As you know, Mr. Hudson has had to pass it
on to me . . . for the moment. . . .

(MRS GARNSEY *looks slightly alarmed.*)

Well, he had to see counsel this morning and
he also thought it might be a good idea if you
were to see me sometime.

53

MRS. G: I see.

BILL: The adultery seems quite clearly established. There are these three women, apart from all the others, there, there seems to be more than enough there. You *have* made a claim for maintenance and alimony. Two children, that's right isn't it?

MRS. G: Do you think I should?

BILL: Mr. Hudson's already advised you, hasn't he?

MRS. G: Yes.

(*Pause.*)

BILL: Mrs. Garnsey. I can tell you what the law is, and on the basis of what you tell me, and on the assumption that what you tell me—is the truth—as best you know it, I can advise you what the legal possibilities are. The rest is up to you.

MRS. G: Yes. That's what Mr. Hudson said to me. It's the law. And——

(*Pause.*)

BILL: Perhaps Mr. Hudson hasn't. . . . Would you like to tell me how you feel? About the whole question. I mean——

(*She nods dumbly.*)

—the first question is always: Why doesn't the marriage work?

(*Silence.*)

Is it: the women? Only? When I say *only*, as far as the law is concerned, that's quite enough.

MRS. G: I don't know. I still don't know what to do. You see, he's a good man really. He's kind, he's very sensitive indeed, he seems to be one step ahead of me all the time in everything, everything. He always has been. He loves me. I know that. . . . I think we. . . . Well, I . . .

54

disappoint him. But no more than he
disappoints himself. . . . You've got all that
stuff that Mr. Hudson took down?
(BILL *nods*.)
He *is* clever, he does his job well. He works
hard. He's good looking. He has a lot of charm,
in his own way, he really has, he can make you
laugh like almost no one else. But what, what
kills me is that he is being hurt so much.

BILL: How do you mean?

MRS. G: By everyone. He comes home to me, and I
know that nothing really works for him. Not
at the office, not his friends, not even his girls.
I wish they would. God knows, he tries hard
enough. I wish I could help him. But I can't,
and everyone, everyone, wherever, we go
together, whether it's a night out, or an
evening at our club, or an outing with the
children, everyone's, I know, everyone's
drawing away from him. And the more people
have been good and kind and thoughtful to
me, the worse it's been for him. I know. And
now. Now: *I'm* doing the same thing. The
children hardly notice him. And now it's *me*.
I can't bear to see him rejected and laughed
at and scorned behind his back and ignored—
(*All this last is scarcely audible*.)
And now it's *me*. I've got to leave him.
(*Nothing more meaningful comes from her*.
BILL *gets up to comfort her but is paralysed*.)

BILL: Joy!
(*Silence but for* MRS. GARNSEY.)
Joy! Joy!
(JOY *appears, surprised*.)
Mrs Garnsey isn't feeling very well. Would

55

you take her and give her a brandy? There's
some in Mr. Hudson's cabinet.

(JOY *supports* MRS. GARNSEY *and takes her out*.)

And get me Mrs. Eaves.

JOY: O.K.

BILL: The minute you can.

(*They go out*. BILL *takes three more pills*.)

Joy!

JOY: (*voice*.) Yes?

BILL: Where's that call?

JOY: No reply.

BILL: What, engaged or no reply?

JOY: No reply.

BILL: Try again. Now!

(*He waits*.)

JOY: (*presently*.) Still no reply.

BILL: Oh. How's Mrs. Garnsey?

JOY: I gave her a whisky. There wasn't any brandy.
She's getting a taxi home.

BILL: Well, get it for her.

JOY: O.K.

BILL: And Joy——

JOY: Well?

BILL: Come in a minute, will you? Now.

(*She comes in*.)

Close the door a minute.

(*She does so*.)

How are you?

JOY: I'm all right. You don't look so hot.

BILL: Joy.

JOY: Yes?

BILL: Will you stay on a bit tonight?

JOY: Is it important?

BILL: Yes.

JOY: If you like.

56

BILL: Thank you.
    (JOY *turns to go.*)
JOY: What shall I do about Mrs. Eaves?
BILL: Keep trying her.
JOY: Will you speak to her?
BILL: No. But. Say I'll be round this evening.
JOY: What time?
BILL: Tell her: to expect me when she sees me.

CURTAIN

End of Act One

ACT TWO

*The same scene. A little grey light. An early morning taxi
can be heard.* BILL *is lying asleep on the sofa, his collar open,
an overcoat over him. He seems to be making an effort to
wake as he did in Act I, and the struggle becomes gradually
more frantic as he tries to escape. He is rescued by the telephone ringing. His eyes open and relief and fatigue mingle as
he sits up. Then apprehension, more than apprehension. He
goes to the telephone on his desk, looks at it. Peers at his
watch. Can't see. Draws the curtains and some light comes
in. He looks out, switches on his desk light and examines his
watch. Cautiously he picks up the telephone. It has not been
put through from the switchboard. He goes into the outer
office and picks up the one on* HUDSON's *desk. The ringing
stops. Quiet.*

BILL: (*presently*). Yes? (*Pause.*) Hello? (*Pause.*) Who is
　　　it? Who's there?
　　　(*The line is dead and he replaces the receiver. He
　　　fumbles with the switchboard, muttering . . .*)
　　　. . . How do you put this . . . thing through!
　　　(*He walks back into his room, picks up the receiver.
　　　Obviously nothing. Goes back to the switchboard.
　　　Returns with a glass of water, picks up the receiver
　　　again. All right this time. He gets his pills out of
　　　his desk drawer, and starts to dial a number. Then
　　　loses courage or strength and puts the receiver
　　　down. He takes one pill which makes him 'gag', as*

58

if he were in a dentist's chair. He goes out for
some soda water, fills a glass, looks at the two pills
to come and re-dials.)

NOTE:

*This telephone conversation and the ones that follow it,
and some of the duologues should progressively re-
semble the feeling of dream and unreality of* BILL's
*giving 'evidence' at the Beginning of Act 1. Some of the
time it should all seem actually taking place at the particular moment, naturally, casual, lucid, unclouded. At
others the grip of the dream grows tighter; for example,
in the call that follows now, the presence of the person on
the other end should be made very real indeed, but, sometimes it should trail off into a feeling of doubt as to
whether there is anyone to speak to at all.*

BILL: (*on phone.*) Liz? Darling? Did I wake you? . . .
I'm sorry . . . it wasn't you ringing then. . .
a few minutes ago . . . I wasn't sure who it
was. . . . Oh—I guess it must have been Anna.
Yes, I'm at the office. . . . Well, it's not like
your own bed, as they say. . . . Yes . . . like a
gimlet, the old thing, right up there behind the
eyeballs. . . . How are *you*? Did you take a
sleeping pill? . . . Three? You're crazy! . . . I
know, my darling, I'm sorry. . . . Yes, I should
have 'phoned, I should have 'phoned. . . .
(*He starts to take his pill with soda water.*)
Just a minute. . . . That's two. . . . That's
three. . . . Sorry . . . I know I said I'd come
round. . . . Oh, come off it, anyway, Shirley
walked out yesterday. . . Well, I'm not surprised
either . . . I know. . . . Yes, well it worried me
too. . . . What do you mean Joy can do the job
just as well? Look, it's too early for jokes and

59

suspicion. . . . Look, hang on just one minute.
(*He claps a hand to his mouth*). Just one minute.
Hang on.
He disappears into the outer office. Sound of
lavatory cistern. He comes back, wiping his face.
Sorry. What? No, I just lost my pills that's
all. . . . Yes, now I'll have to take three more. . .
I made a mistake, I just had plain water with
the first one. . . . Look, I know I should have
phoned but I didn't and I couldn't. But I love
you dearly and I wanted to be with you and
talk to you more than anything. . . . Well, I'll
tell you what happened . . . only no more jolly,
barbed jokes about Joy. Please . . . I know, but
I'm allowed to make them. . . . All right, I won't
make them any more. . . . It was a bad day,
Liz, a bad day right from the beginning. . . . I
was just about to ring you because I reckoned
on having a good three quarters of an hour
before meeting Anna. . . . Well, there was a lot
of work in. . . . Anyhow, she turned up here
suddenly at seven thirty. . . . No, the downstairs
door was locked. . . . Well the caretaker always
does that. . . . No, she didn't. . . . Darling, I
said please no more Joy jokes. . . . Well, what
could I do? I couldn't ring you with her here in
the room. . . . Well, I know it doesn't make any
difference at this stage, but I couldn't bring
myself to do it. . . . I don't think you'd have
cared much for the experience either. . . . She'd
arranged for us to go out to these dreary friends
of hers, the Watsons . . . that's right, they're the
ones, they write books together . . . Sociology
and Sex. I don't know—Natural Childbirth and
C.N.D.: An Analysis. . . . All tables and diagrams

and unreadable. . . . Yes. All it adds up to in the
end is either do it or don't. We do. . . . You've
got it. Every time she drops one he's in there in
the room with a surgical mask on and popping
away with his camera. . . . Yes . . . being
encouraging. . . . Well, it's pretty discouraging to
look at them together. . . . Oh, sure, *rotten*
dinner. . . . Oh, wooden bowls, yes, sort of
Sunday Times Supplement Primitive. . . *very*
badly cooked. . . . Hullo. . . . Hullo. . . . Are
you there? . . . Oh. . . . I keep thinking you're
not there. . . . Well, you weren't saying
anything and I suddenly. . . . Hullo. . . .
Hullo. . . . Oh, hell's bloody bells. . . . Well, as
I say she turned up here. . . . I know, well it's
not something you'd do. . . . You're too clever
for that. . . . Well I didn't just mean. . . . She
pitched into the weekend thing the minute I
answered the door. . . . Yes—Joy answered the
door. . . . No, I think that quite pleased her.
She felt if anything had been going on you'd
have been the loser and not her. . . . Which is
kind of true. . . . I had a drink, and told her
the truth. . . just that: that that you and I
hadn't had any time together for weeks and we
were determined to have at least three whole,
clear, uncluttered days together—and Jane, well
just bad luck. She's a nice girl but she's a
strapping nevertheless seventeen, less than half
our age and looked after and cosseted and God
knows what. Besides she's young, she's got all
that youth everyone's so mad about and
admires. Even if she's not very clever or pretty,
she's got good old youth. I'd never use anything
else if I could help it. . . . Sure, she'll not get

61

into any mess like us. . . . Hullo. . . . Hullo. . . .
I say, like *us*. Or, if she does, it won't matter,
it won't overwhelm her or get the better of
her. . . . I promise you that's what I said. . . .
Yes. . . . I said we just had to go. . . . I love
you very dearly. . . . Yes, I did say it. . . . Oh,
what's the matter? I don't seem to hear
properly. . . . Yes, we went to the party, don't
ask me why, I think I'd even have rather gone
home. . . . Of course I had too much booze,
what do you think. . . . It was strange, as if I
were there on tolerance. . . . Sure, they're sorry
for Anna and think I'm a boorish old ram but
it was more, there was more to it than that. . . .
I don't know. . . . Liz. . . . Liz. . . . Hullo,
Liz. . . . I'm frightened. . . . It was as if I only
existed because of her, because she allowed me
to, but if she turned off the switch . . . turned
off the switch . . . who knows? But if she'd
turned it off I'd have been dead. . . . They
would have passed me by like a blank hoarding
or a tombstone, or waste ground by the railway
line or something. . . . And then there was Mrs.
Garnsey. . . . Mrs. Garnsey, you remember
her . . . I don't know what to do about her. . . .
No, quite straightforward really. . . . Of course
we will. What did I have the row about then?
She knows all about it. Not that she didn't
anyway. . . . Believe me. . . . Oh, there was a
sort of row at the table and we left early. . . .
Sure, she wanted to stay. . . . I took her home
and, oh, it went on and I came back here. The
car was in the garage, I couldn't get a taxi, so I
came back and slept here. . . . I wanted to, but
I didn't want to break in on you somehow. . . .

I know I should have but I couldn't! Well. . . .
Look, I'll come over the minute I can. I'm
longing to see you and I can't wait and I'm
dreading today. . . . Well, I'll make a hole in
the day. . . . Hullo. . . . Hullo. . . . Stay in
won't you? Stay in, I'll ring you. 'Bye.
(*He puts the phone down. Picks it up again
several times to see if it is alive. Gets out a
razor, brush and mirror and looks at them dully.
Dials phone again.*)

(*More than ever the ambiguity of reality is
marked, of whether the phone is dead, of whether
the person at the other end exists. He trails back
and forth between lucidity and near off-handedness
and fumbling and fear and addressing himself.*)

(*Some jokes are addressed to himself, some
bravado is deflated to himself, some is dialogue
between real people. The telephone is stalked,
abused, taken for granted, feared. Most of all the
fear of being cut off, of no sound from either end.*)

BILL: (*on phone*). Anna? How are you? . . . I'm
sorry. . . . Didn't you take a pill? . . . Well, it's
hardly surprising then, is it? . . . You rang
me . . . oh, my dear, come off it, of course I
know it was you. You've got your own
click. . . . No, I spent the night here, believe it
or not. . . I couldn't get a taxi so I walked
here . . . you obviously rang up to find out
where I am not *how* I am. . . . Oh, great,
especially after your little visit and then your
friends . . . well, it wasn't exactly a load of old
fun was it? . . . Well, *you* were a success, but
then you always are . . . I didn't mean it

63

unkindly, you deserve to be. It's just that the
more they despise me the more admirable and
courageous and decent spirited you become. . . .
Sometimes I think you're my only grip left, if
you let me go, I'll disappear, I'll be made to
disappear, nothing will work, I'll be like
something in a capsule in space, weightless,
unable to touch anything or do anything, like
a groping baby in a removed, putrefying
womb. . . . No, I'll not leave you. . . . I've told
you. I'll not leave you . . . *you* are leaving me
. . . I told you the weekend is out, it's out, the
weekend is out. . . . Yes, I am. . . . I don't
know about Liz. She may be the last to pack it
in, but pack it in she will. . . . Of course she's
coming with me. . . because I haven't seen her
probably for six bloody weeks and I have to be
with her. . . . I know I am, have I ever denied
it. . . . I see Jane every day of the week and no
one could be more relieved to be rid of me
when her friends are around. . . because I'm
only an inquisitive, hostile, undistinguished
square I suppose, and I bore the jeans off her. . .
must you always say 'mistress'? It's a very
melodramatic word for a very commonplace
archetype . . . you make it sound like a
pterodactyl who gives you lung cancer . . . or
something. . . . Yes, well she said something
almost identical about you—with a little more
wit, I may say. . . . Well, she's quite a
a humorous girl. . . . Oh, something about
your gold lamé hairstyle . . . and, oh yes, your
dress: what did she call it: chintz and sequin
collage. . . . I don't know, someone must have
described it to her—no—not me. . . . Well,

you're neither of you the greatest dressers in
the world . . . I know, but mistresses, as you
call them, are usually less tolerant than wives.
Mind you, they're also less patronizing but
totally without generosity. . . . No, I malign her
about that. . . . Yes, and you too. Look, has
Jane left yet? Could you put her on . . . I want
to speak to her, that's why. . . . Listen, I'm a
fairly rotten father but better than some, at
least I can ask my daughter a question on the
telephone. After all, she can refuse to speak to
me if she wants to. But try not to prompt her?
(*Pause*.)
Jane? Hullo, darling, how are you? . . . I
should say I'm more or less the same as
usual. Or, rather less than usual. How's the
Drama then? I don't mean your personal
drama, if you have one, I mean speech training
and improvisation or whatever it is? . . . Good,
well I'm glad. You deserve it. You see, you'll
you'll be a dame before I die. No, well by the
time you're thirty. . . . What I wanted to ask is
could you pop in and see me today? . . . This
morning, any time? . . . No, it's not all that
important, but I'm just asking you if you would
do me a favour and give me ten minutes of your
time . . . we could have lunch if you'd . . . well,
can't you cut voice production or something?
You speak quite beautifully enough as it is. . . .
I'm not flattering you—or bribing you. Frankly
that folk song and Poetry Recital voice gives
me the flaming pip, I'm just asking you to see
me for a few minutes at least before. . . . That's
better! I'll buy you an air cushion for the next
Aldermaston. Save you getting felt up in

Trafalgar Square too. . . . Sorry, well, it *is*
nine o'clock in the morning and my sofa isn't
very comfortable. . . . Thank you, darling, very
much. It won't take. . . . What? All right, put
her on.
(*Pause.*)
Hullo. . . . I honestly don't know. . . . No, I
really don't. It's a bit of a tough day. Hudson
seems to be in court all the time nowadays.
Jones is useless . . . well, the truth is I don't like
him then; it's all right him working for me, but
I'd feel differently if he wanted to marry my
daughter. I just hope to God she wouldn't want
to. . . . Of course I'm not drunk, a little of last
night's fire is coursing through the gates and
natural alleys of the body with my three pills,
that's all. Anyway, Jane's sure to marry an
emergent African. Perhaps I am a bit, I don't
know. That is, if she hasn't already sent her
virginity to OXFAM. . . . I tell you I don't know.
I've got to see Mrs. Garnsey again. I'm going
to fail there, I've done it already, but she's
coming in again to lose her grip or whatever it
is, and then there's Tonks and Tonks and an
indecent assault or criminal assault I don't
remember which, and some bank manager
who's a flasher and. . . . Yes, I am seeing her,
you must know that, you *do* know that, now. . .
I'll let you know and I'll come back . . . as soon
as I can. . . . I know you do. . . . I love you.
. . . It just doesn't do much good does it? . . .
Look, try and take a pill and go back to bed
. . . O.K., please yourself. Oh, don't talk Jane
out of coming to see me. No, forget it. If you
can and you want to, well. . . . 'Bye.

(*He puts the phone down. There is a noise from
the outer office. He calls out:*
Joy.
(*No reply. He gets up, looks through the door.
There is no one there. He comes back, looks at
at his watch. Picks up phone, dials. Waits. No
reply. He waits, then looks carefully at his
thumb. Puts down the phone. Not knowing what
to precipitate next. Again, a noise from the outer
office. Someone has certainly come in this time.
He waits. No one appears and he can't bear it
any longer.*
Joy? Joy?
(HUDSON *appears, taking off his raincoat. He
takes in the sofa-bed and situation.*)

HUDSON: (*ponderously, of course.*) Hullo—early bird.

BILL: Oh.

HUDSON: Where's the woman, then?

BILL: Flown.

HUDSON: How was she?

BILL: Fine.

HUDSON: Well, that's good.

BILL: Sure. Let me tell you, she could lose you in five
minutes.

HUDSON: Delighted to hear it.

BILL: Tell me, what about Shirley?

HUDSON: What about her?

BILL: Do you think she'll come back?

HUDSON: No. You've seen the last of her.

BILL: Really? The last?

HUDSON: She rang Joy and asked her to send her cards
off last night.
(*Another noise from outer office.*)

BILL: If that's Jones, keep him out of my way, I
don't want to see him.

HUDSON: Well—sounds as if you've met your match this time.

BILL: What do you mean?

HUDSON: Perhaps you'd better take the day off.

BILL: I've too much to do.

HUDSON: What have you done to your thumb?

BILL: I keep looking at it, that's all. It's rather painful. But they're rather interesting to look at, anyway. I never did look at it properly before. Have you? I wonder if it's cancer. (JONES *looks in.*)

JONES: Hullo.

HUDSON: Hullo. Come on your scooter?

JONES: Yes.

HUDSON: Well, you'd better go and thaw out I should think.

JONES: No Shirley then?

HUDSON: No. Not any more.

JONES: Where's Joy?

HUDSON: Overslept we believe.

JONES: Well, I'll do the post then.

HUDSON: Yes, I should if I were you.

JONES: What's that?

HUDSON: The boss has got cancer this morning.

JONES: Oh?

HUDSON: In his thumb. (JONES *goes out.*)

BILL: Thank God for that. I suppose you're in court all day again.

HUDSON: 'Fraid so.

BILL: Why do you leave it all to me?

HUDSON: What would you like me to do?

BILL: I don't know.

HUDSON: You've got Jones.

BILL: Thanks. You can take him with you.

68

HUDSON: Well, I'd better leave you then. Oh, how did you get on with Mrs. Garnsey?

BILL: Didn't work out at all.

HUDSON: I didn't think it would.

BILL: Eh?

HUDSON: We got the husband's reply in after she'd left.

BILL: Well?

HUDSON: Oh. I don't think she's got anything to worry about.

(BILL *stares at him and starts to laugh. Another noise in the outer office.*)

HUDSON: That'll be Joy.

BILL: Send her in.

HUDSON: Right.

BILL: Wally—have you thought any more about my offer? (*Pause.*) The offer, Wally. The Partnership.

HUDSON: Yes. As a matter of fact I have given it a bit of thought.

BILL: And?

HUDSON: I'd like to take a bit more time over it. If you don't mind.

BILL: And Piffards?

HUDSON: They don't seem to be in any hurry for a decision.

BILL: No? Well, they're a big firm. Right, well then. (*Pause.*) Joy!

(*She appears.*)

HUDSON: Ah, there she is.

JOY: D'you want me?

HUDSON: Bright as a button.

BILL: Bring in the post, will you?

JOY: Mr. Jones is sorting it.

BILL: Well, bring in what he's done.

JOY: O.K.

BILL: And ring Mrs. Garnsey.

JOY: Which?

BILL: Which what?

JOY: Which first?

BILL: Oh—Mrs. Garnsey. I want to catch her.
(*She nods and goes out*.)

HUDSON: You sound as though you think you'd lost her.
Well, see you later.
(*He goes out.* BILL *reaches for the intercom*.)

BILL: Joy! Get me Mrs. Eaves.

JOY: Which?

BILL: What? Oh, you speak to Mrs. Garnsey. Make
another appointment for her as soon as she can.

JOY: O.K.

BILL: And what about Shirley?

JOY: What about her?

BILL: Well, isn't she coming in?

JOY: Why should she?

BILL: You mean she's really left?

JOY: Yes. Really.
(BILL *stares at his thumb. The phone rings*.)

BILL: (*on phone*.) Liz? Look, I'm sorry. It's just that
it's going to be a day. I can see it only too
well. . . . Yes, I'm all right. My thumb's a bit
painful, that's all. . . . Yes, of course it's
cancer. But, look, you will stay in, won't you.
Whatever happens, wait for me, don't leave
will you? O.K. Thank you. . . . But you won't
leave. . . . 'Bye.
(JOY *reappears with some letters*.)

JOY: This is all for the moment. You know how slow
he is.

BILL: O.K. Give them here. Did you get Mrs.
Garnsey?

JOY: Well, I spoke to someone. Her sister or
someone.

BILL: Close the door.
    (*She does so.*)
JOY: She said she'd changed her mind.
BILL: Changed her mind?
JOY: That's what she said.
BILL: But did you make it clear it was important I see
    her again?
JOY: Sure. She just said would you send in the
    account.
BILL: But I wanted to see her again.
    (*Pause.*)
JOY: Shall I send it in then?
BILL: What? Oh, yes, I suppose so. No. No, don't.
JOY: But that's crazy.
BILL: How are you this morning?
JOY: I'm fine.
BILL: Well, you look it, I must say.
JOY: Thank you, Mr. Maitland.
BILL: Did you get home all right?
JOY: Well, it was only half past seven in the evening,
    you know. I didn't exactly have a night out.
BILL: I'm sorry.
JOY: For what? We enjoyed ourselves. Didn't we?
BILL: Yes, I think we did.
JOY: The draught under that door's a bit much,
    though. And it was a bit of a shock opening the
    door to your old woman.
BILL: But you don't regret it?
JOY: Maybe there'll be other times, other places. And
    if not, well. . . . She's very attractive, isn't she?
BILL: Do you think so?
JOY: Well, don't you?
BILL: Yes. Yes. I do. So many of you are.
JOY: I've only one regret, but that's more or less the
    usual one.

71

BILL: What's that then?

JOY: Bill.

BILL: Yes, Joy?

JOY: I have one flaw in my character. Well, not just one, but one that crops up all the time. You see I want to have sex constantly, I mean I'm always wanting it, I always have:

BILL: Joy: for a woman to make that admission is no shame, believe you me.

JOY: Ah, but everyone tells you differently. Right? You lose a man's respect, you lose your own sense of respect and all that old load of rubbish. Right?

BILL: Right.

JOY: So. So I've always felt guilty. There it is, daft, but I am. So I have to get them to say 'I love you'. And then, then I say 'I love you'.

BILL: And then?

JOY: And then. Then: I feel better. (*Pause.*) You see.

BILL: I'm sorry.

JOY: Don't be. You don't love me. And I don't love you. But it's all right. Isn't it?
(*She kisses him lightly.*)
You're a funny old thing. You're scared aren't you?

BILL: Yes.

JOY: Well, Joy won't leave you. Not yet a while. What do you want doing?

BILL: I don't know. Just cope, will you?

JOY: Sure.

BILL: There's this Tonks thing. And that boy. The indecent assault. Or was it criminal?

JOY: Shall I ask Mr. Jones?

BILL: No. Just hang on to that switchboard.

JOY: All right, love.

BILL: Oh, my daughter's coming in.

JOY: When?

BILL: Sometime this morning. Just send her right in.

JOY: O.K. See you later.

(*She goes out.*)

BILL: (*calls out.*) Oh, try and see if you can get Mrs.
Garnsey personally, and I'll talk to her. If not,
if not remind me to send a letter.

(*Presently* JONES *looks in.*)

BILL: Well?

JONES: Joy told me to bring in the rest.

BILL: Great.

JONES: There's not a great deal.

BILL: Not a great deal. Any money in? Any business?
Any problems?

(JONES *looks dull.*)

JONES: Only what you see there. Mr. Hudson told me
to sort it out for you.

BILL: Sort it out? Yes, I'll bet. Do you think old
Wally's going to leave us?

JONES: No idea. Except he's had an offer from
Piffards.

BILL: What do you think about that?

JONES: Well, they're a very respected firm. Aren't they?

BILL: Very.

JONES: Not much criminal stuff.

BILL: No.

JONES: Libel, isn't it?

BILL: Quite a lot. Would you like that?

JONES: What—libel? Not specially.

BILL: What would you like specially?

JONES: Oh, I don't know. It's all much the same when
you come down to it, isn't it?

BILL: But if they—Piffards—offered you a job, you'd
take it, wouldn't you?

JONES: Well, I, I'm not likely to be asked, at this stage, anyway, am I?

BILL: No.

(*Pause.*)

JONES: Have I done something wrong?

BILL: No, nothing. I admit I've tried to catch you out. But usually, you come round. Even if it takes a little time. You're pretty solid, I'd say. Solid but forward looking, you know, a child of the jet age, a new age of fulfilment with streamlined institutions, a sense of purpose and looking forward to the new frontiers of knowledge. If Mr. Hudson leaves, do you think you could take his place?

JONES: I don't know. I might.

BILL: But you might not. You might go elsewhere?

JONES: Well, I haven't had a lot of experience yet, and it doesn't do any harm to strike out a bit—

BILL: That's right. I think you should. What's this?

JONES: Tonks v. Tonks. Anderson v. Anderson and Maples. Oh, and that's the supplemental petition.

BILL: What's Maples?

JONES: Indecent assault.

BILL: Well, what are you giving him to me for?

JONES: Well, Mr. Hudson thought you'd be better to deal with this one.

BILL: Yes, I see. Has this been sent to counsel?

JONES: Mr. Hudson said you might like to have a word with Mr. Winters about it, but he said he didn't think he'd touch it.

BILL: He'll touch it if I ask him.

(*Disbelief between them.*)

JONES: Well, if you like, I can give them to Mr. Winters this morning.

BILL: No, I'll do it. But I'll see Maples first.
Otherwise, if you send him straight down to
Winters, he'll carve him up. What do you make
of him?

JONES: Maples? Not much.

BILL: Oh?

JONES: Well, he hums and hahs. And stammers.

BILL: Perhaps he's nervous. At being prosecuted by
the police.

JONES: But he's a bit affected at the same time.

BILL: Does he seem like a pouf?

JONES: (*casually*.) Yes. I should say so.

BILL: Do you believe him?

JONES: Well, it's a bit fishy, isn't it?

BILL: Yes.

JONES: I mean, put him up before old Glover, and I
wouldn't give him much chance. First offender
and all, six months.

BILL: We'll just hope the old bastard breaks a leg. I
don't think he's ever missed a day yet though.
Sir Watkin Glover, V.C. For Vicious Character.

JONES: And then there's Mr. Simley.

BILL: Who's that? Oh, yes, the bank manager who's
a flasher. Perhaps I can do something for
Maples. What time's he due?

JONES: Eleven.

BILL: Try not to let me keep him waiting.

JONES: I'm going out.

BILL: Oh, yes. Well, tell Joy. All we want is one good
reliable person.

JONES: What?

BILL: A witness?

JONES: Oh.

BILL: There isn't one is there?

JONES: No.

75

BILL: Well, we'll see. I like the sound of Maples. Better than I like Piffards. Ask Joy to get me a glass of water.

JONES: O.K.

BILL: Most of these police jobs are decided by someone quite outside the event. They're not the only ones who can 'lean' on the evidence. You think someone's going to shop me to the Law Society one day, don't you? Someone will send an anonymous little note, and I'll get a summons to defend my professional conduct. I wonder who it'll be. Someone's sure to do it. It's surprising it's not happened before. I've been threatened with it, you see. Someone at Piffards actually. He never did. I don't know why. Milson it was, not the old man, he wouldn't have bothered with me. The young one, I wonder who it will be though. Someone—
(*Pause.*)

JONES: I hear you've lost Mrs. Garnsey.

BILL: What do you mean *I've* lost Mrs. Garnsey?

JONES: Well, *we've* lost Mrs. Garnsey. The firm has.

BILL: The *firm* has? I'm writing her a letter. Something went wrong. I scared her off. In some way. I could feel her withdrawing from me. I'm the wrong man for these things. You and Hudson should do them. *You're* the right people. You can handle them—I can't. They turn away from me, and they're probably right. (*He looks at the papers on his desk.*)
And you really can't, either of you, do these?

JONES: You know what we've got in. Well, I'll get on. You wanted a glass of water. O.K.?

BILL: When are you getting married?

JONES: Don't know yet. I haven't really made up my

76

mind. Still, there's no hurry. About these things.
Is there?

BILL: No. Not if you don't feel it.

(JONES *goes out.* BILL *picks up a divorce petition
and starts reading in a low voice:*)

In the High Court of Justice, Probate Divorce
and Admiralty Division. Divorce. To the High
Court of Justice the 27th day of January 1964.
The humble petition of Maureen Sheila Tonks.
Maureen. I remember Maureen. She always,
well not always, but most times I went out with
her, wore hand knitted suits, knitted by her
mother. They'd always shrink and they were in
horrible colours and her skirts would be too
short because of it, which worried her. It
worried me, but she always seemed to be in
some pain, some funny pain, *physical* pain I
mean. It was never any good. Which was a pity
because she has the most strange blue eyes with
dark hair, very dark. English beauty her mother
called it. English beauty. And Sheila. Well I
remember two of them. One was Scots with
white, flaky skin. She rode a bicycle with a
crossbar and didn't give a damn. She'd punch
and go at you like a boy, but she'd cry too
when it came to it.

JOY: (*entering.*) Mrs Tonks to see you.

BILL: (*rises.*) Ah, Good morning.

(MRS. TONKS *enters. It is the same woman as*
MRS. GARNSEY. *Played by the same actress.*)

BILL: Please sit down. Would you like some tea or
coffee?

MRS. TONKS: No, thank you very much.

BILL: Right. Thank you, Joy.

(JOY *goes out.*)

77

Right. Now. I'll just give this to you, if you'd care to look at it. I want you to go over it very carefully. It's your petition, the smaller one is the supplemental petition. Mr. Hudson's just prepared it so there may be one or two things— (*pause.*) All right?

MRS. T: (*she nods presently.*) (*She begins.*) The humble petition of Maureen Sheila Tonks. That. On the twenty first day of April 1958, your petitioner Maureen Sheila Tonks, then Maureen Sheila Williams, Spinster, was lawfully married to Richard George Tonks, hereinafter called the respondent, at the Parish Church of St. Hilda's in the County Borough of Leicester. That. After the said marriage, your petitioner and the respondent lived and cohabited at divers addresses and from October 1960 to August 1963 or thereabouts at 42 Macwilliam Street.

BILL: Lived and cohabited.

MRS. T: Save and except that in the application of the petitioner by reason of the respondent's cruelty, the Justices of the Petty Sessional Division of Kingston did on the 12th day of August 1963 make an order that the petitioner be no longer bound to cohabit, to live with and cohabit, with the respondent and that he should pay her a weekly sum of two pounds seventeen shillings.

BILL: Skip on to paragraph nine.
(*She fumbles.*)
There.

MRS. T: That. That the respondent is a man of excessive sexual appetite who has habitually and constantly made sexual demands on the petitioner which he knew she regarded as

78

inordinate or revolting.

BILL: Habitually and constantly. I'm sorry. . . . In your husband's answers, which, admittedly aren't very coherent, he says. Now. Paras one to seven correct. Para eight I deny that I have been cruel to my wife. Here we are, paragraph nine: I deny being a man of excessive sexual appetite. There were never sexual relations between us except by mutual agreement. (*Pause.*) Are you all right?
(*She nods.*)
Right, let's get on then.

MRS. T: That. On many occasions, occasions insisted on having intercourse three times and even four times a day. He adopted a practice he termed
. . . .

BILL: Paragraph twelve, your husband says the allegations contained are a gross exaggeration of the true facts.

MRS. T: That the respondent refused to cease from having intercourse during the time of the petitioner's menstrual periods at 42 Macwilliam Street and number 11 Wicker Street, notwithstanding the petitioner's entreaties. . . .

BILL: There were difficulties between us. Such that my wife failed to reach satisfaction.

MRS. T: That. On frequent occasions at the said addresses whilst he was having intercourse with petitioner he did. . . .

BILL: My wife visited the Marriage Guidance Council on at least three occasions who told her they believed the difficulty was due to my wife's reluctance. . . .

MRS. T: Notwithstanding the fact that he knew the

petitioner found this conduct revolting and
upsetting.

BILL: We've none of us been reluctant much have we?
Well, there were girls like Maureen, and even
with you there were difficulties but not revolting
or upsetting. At least, not much, I don't think
so. You weren't reluctant, you should be happy,
you didn't cling on to it like it was the crown
jewels. You were generous, loving, bright, you
should have been able to cope. *I* should have
been able to cope.

MRS. T: He told the petitioner he liked to hear the noise
made by. . . .

BILL: To have another child. Another child. In spite
of the advice given to her by the Counsel she
refused to use this.

MRS. T: That. It was his desire to have sexual
intercourse with a woman in this street to
whom he referred. . . .

BILL: Because she said it was nasty. Nasty and messy.

MRS. T: He constantly referred to as "that great big
beautiful blonde bat.'

BILL: I wonder if it was real or dyed. Not that it
matters.

MRS. T: On at least eleven occasions during the marriage
he attempted to commit. . . .

BILL: I deny that I persisted.

MRS. T: And did in fact.

BILL: There is no truth at all in this.

MRS. T: Upon the person of the petitioner, compelling
the petitioner with force to submit.

BILL: I repected my wife's feelings at all times and
especially. . . .

MRS. T: To these malpractices. That. In March 1961
when the petitioner was seven months

pregnant with the child Laura, the respondent
violently chastised the child Edward with a
heavy brush of a type. . . .

BILL: No truth at all in these allegations. . . .

MRS. T: After the said occurrence on the 19th July
1961. . . .

BILL: As described, bears no relation to what actually
happened. I do admit there were many times
when I failed. Many times.

MRS. T: The petitioner left the respondent.

BILL: I failed in giving her complete satisfaction. My
wife left me on the 12th day of September 1963.

MRS TONKS: Wherefore your petitioner humbly prays
that the court will exercise its discretion in her
favour and decree (1) That. The said marriage
may be dissolved. (2) That. She may be granted
the custody of the children of the said marriage.
(3) That. The respondent be condemned in the
costs of the proceedings.

BILL: All the time we have lived together she has been
a very highly strung person. She has been
constantly depressed and been to the doctor, but
it all seems to have come to no good. I have done
all I can. Signed: Richard George Tonks.
(*Pause*.)
(JOY *enters*.)

JOY: I'm sorry, but Mrs Anderson is downstairs. What
do you want me to do?

BILL: Has Mr. Jones gone yet?

JOY: He's just leaving.

BILL: Well, stop him. He can't leave yet. Not yet.
We need. . . Mrs. Tonks, would you mind going
into the other room? I think you've met Mr.
Jones. There are one or two things to be sorted
out here, and, we really ought to get on with

them. All right?

(*She smiles.*)

I've just got someone else to see. You'll be
looked after. You'll be looked after. It's *not* a
question of passing you on. All right? Joy will
look after you. I'm sure you wouldn't mind a
cup of coffee or something now?

(JOY *takes* MRS. TONKS *out.* BILL *picks up another
petition.*)

BILL: Audrey Jane Anderson. Audrey, I remember
Audrey. Even an Audrey Jane. I thought she
was a bit posh. Except she wasn't. She just took
elocution and dancing and wore patent shoes.
I think. I'm not sure, I thought I could
remember. And I've no idea of what's to come.
I can't even call to mind little details like that. If
only it could be fixed. And improved. Improved.
But it doesn't, nothing does. I can't even
re-assemble it. Why do I do it? Well, not
because it's good. I suppose: I suppose: because
it still has a little withered ball of interest.
Somewhere. Audrey Jane Anderson. The returns
are coming in and they aren't good.

(JOY *enters with* MRS. ANDERSON *Again it is the
same woman as* MRS. GARNSEY, *as* MRS. TONKS.)

BILL: Ah. Please sit down. Would you like some tea
or coffee?

MRS. ANDERSON: No thank you.

BILL: All right. Thank you, Joy.

(JOY *goes out.*)

Right. Now. I'll just give this to you. Mrs.
Anderson. If you'd like to take a look at it. It's
just a rough, rough summary of the statement
Mr. Jones, Mr. Hudson took down for you. So
I'm sure there'll be one or two things to clear

up. All right?

(*She nods.*)

Good. Carry on then.

MRS. A: Audrey Jane Anderson will prove as follows:

BILL: What goes wrong? Nothing happens for you, I fail you, and you're frightened and full of dislike.

MRS. A: I was married at Kidderminster Registry Office. I was a spinster. My maiden name was Wall. My husband was then a clerk in the local post office. Our marriage—

BILL: Our marriage. What a phrase.

MRS. A: Our marriage seemed normal for a time and reasonably happy. There were difficulties owing to the fact that we were living at my mother's house, 148 Chadacre Road, for two years.

(BILL *makes a massive effort to assemble the facts in his mind. It is very difficult.*

BILL: Two years. You know, you mustn't expect people to behave well towards you, Audrey. You mustn't. I know you have and I know you will.

MRS. ANDERSON: There was discord when I was pregnant with the little boy Patrick John.

BILL: Patrick John.

MRS. A.: My parents persuaded me to return to him.

BILL: You must always ask yourself. Is it dangerous or is it safe? And then make your choice. If you can, if you can.

MRS. A: Things became increasingly unhappy and difficult when my husband gave up his job and became a traveller for a firm in electrical fittings. He was able to be at home most of the time, but when he was away, never more than for the odd day or two, he would accuse me of going

83

out with men.

BILL: Well. She thinks I've got mistresses all over London. They both do. And it's not even true. Worse luck. No, thank God.

MRS. A: He said I ought to go on the streets.

BILL: You might have met me then. You might have been worse off.

MRS. A: I have never been with anyone apart from my husband.

BILL: That's what's wrong with all of you, you dim deluded little loving things. You listen to promiscuous lady journalists and bishops and your mother. And hang on to it.

MRS. A: But he's always saying these things.

BILL: He listens.

MRS. A: It's as if he can't help it. When he wanted to, he would have intercourse two or three times a day. He would, he would go as far as he could but that was all. But it's not only that, it's not even that. If it were only that I could put up with all kinds of things. Because I know he is a good man, really, and a kind man. He can be, and he has been kind to me.

BILL: I love you. He never said, he hardly ever said, he stopped saying, he found it difficult to say I love you. It has to be heaved and dropped into the pool after you, a great rock of I love you, and then you have to duck down below the surface and bring it up, like some gasping, grateful, stupid dog.

MRS. A: He loves the children, and is always making a fuss of them, and giving them things. My sister used to come in to watch T.V., but I hardly ever went out while she was there. We went to the doctor and he made me go to Weymouth for two weeks for a complete rest.

BILL: I often think of my dying. And her, I mean. Of
her being a widow. As opposed to a wife. A
blackened wife. Of the kind of suit she would
wear and wear and where she would get it
from. She hasn't got a useful black suit. Liz has,
but I don't think she'd get there. Which worries
me. Because the idea of her not being there is
disturbing. I've asked her to be there, and she's
promised me, which is damned silly and a lot to
ask, especially if you think of her having to face
Anna in her black suit. I wonder if they'd
notice what the other was wearing. In the
crematorium with all that G-Plan light oak and
electrical department brass fittings and spanking
new magenta hassocks. And the pink curate
sending me off at thirty bob a head as I go
rattling on little rails behind him and disappear
like a truck on the ghost train at Dreamland, in
the Amusement Park, behind the black curtains,
and all the noise.

MRS. A: I am on National Assistance. Three pounds
twelve shillings a week. I am not working now,
not since early May.

BILL: But did you really enjoy work? Did you? You
didn't enjoy sex. Wasn't it just another effort,
um? I mean an effort on your part, some way
of helping, of fighting off what's going to
happen to you?

MRS. A: I'm still under the doctor. The defendant has
given me housekeeping all the time—barring a
short period of about a fortnight. He has not
touched me sexually since August Bank
Holiday. He slept in another room for a few
weeks, but he used to cry quite often and it kept

85

me awake. We would both cry sometimes. He offered to leave me alone. I told him I would leave him if that's what he wanted. I still wanted some happiness for him. We are buying the house and the T.V., has been paid for. He said he would save for the down payment on a car and take us all out—a mini—and take us all out at the weekends to the sea. I am quite sure he meant it. I think he wanted to, I think he really did.

BILL: There was a time when I used to speculate about *her* death. Oh, but not only Anna's. I'd be crunching back up that new path with the planks and the wet clay and the flowers. Perhaps I'd have walked out of that place on my own, there'd have been no one else, I could have done as I liked. I could have sat in Lyons and got myself a cup of coffee and a roll and butter all on my own. I might have looked around me, and my throat would have been tight and I'd have trouble with my coffee, and I'd smile sentimentally at the coloured girl who was clearing away the plates just because she was coloured, and my throat seemed to be closed up with the business of dying, and I'd kid myself we were friendly to one another. I might have gone mad and bought myself a new suit. Something a bit too sharp for someone my age and size, but I'd have stalked into some popular camp store and got something off the peg. And some shirts. I'd make up my mind to throw out all my old shirts and buy new ones, clean cotton shirts with that new smell, and lots of large handkerchiefs. All new. I'd have walked around, trying to remember London, trying to put it together, looking for street musicians with my pockets full of change.

MRS. A: I have often contributed to finance. Often by simply going without new things or buying things cheap from my sister.

BILL: I think I'd have gone on a bus. An eleven or a thirty eight. All the way. Say, from Putney to Hackney.

MRS. A: When he gets in at night after work and early in the morning. Before I get up to get his breakfast.

BILL: I'd have had dinner alone, very, very, slowly. I'd have had a cigar and a Calvados or Marc de Bourgogne. Or—and—or I'd have gone to the pictures or a theatre with no one beside me except my new overcoat and a new book to read at home in bed, a new novel perhaps, by some woman perhaps. Something which might surprise me, take me by surprise a bit. Something I hadn't quite thought of, or not in that way, or so well, or, but not something that necessarily, no, something that didn't disturb me. Perhaps something easier. Something new but old. Something. A fat biography, perhaps something scandalous, about Marshall Hall. Or Rufus Isaacs. Something new.

MRS. A: He says I'm not natural. He says I'm not like a woman should be.

BILL: My death and hers. Theirs? Yours: and mine. Who first? Um?

MRS. A: He says I've no intelligence and no brains and no education. And I'm not fit to run anything, not even a brothel. I have not imagined, imagined any of these things because I may be unhappy or unwell.

(*Her voice is disappearing, but she rallies for her last speech.*)

BILL: Good. Now. Joy!

(JOY *appears.*)

MRS. A: I know I'm no good at all to him. He humiliates me. I know he hates me. I wish I could have done better. That I could go back.

(JOY *touches her shoulder and she follows her out.*)

(*Pause.*)

BILL: Joy!

JOY: Yes.

BILL: Get me Mr. Winters, will you?

JOY: O.K.

BILL: Tell him it's urgent.

JOY: Mr. Maples is downstairs. Shall I send him in?

BILL: No. I want to speak to Winters first. Then afterwards. Did you look after Mrs Tonks?

JOY: She went.

BILL: Went?

JOY: That's right. Well, I'll get Winters.

(*She goes out. Presently her voice comes from his desk.*)

JOY: Mr. Winters in engaged at present.

BILL: Well, of course he is. Hudson's with him isn't he?

JOY: I'll see. (*Pause.*) They say Mr. Hudson's gone.

BILL: What's the matter with them all? Well, put me on to Roberts. (*Pause.*) His managing clerk. Come on. Don't *you* start.

(*Pause.*)

JOY: (*off.*) He's not available.

BILL: Not available! But that's his job: to be available. He doesn't ever have to be anything else.

JOY: Well, that's what they say.

BILL: Here: put me on to them.

JOY: What?

BILL: Put me through! Hullo. Charley! Hullo! What's going on. Can I speak to Mr. Roberts, please? What do you mean? Out? He can't be out. I can hear his voice. . . . I tell you: I can hear his voice. . . . I see. . . . All right. . . . Well, please ask him . . . to ring me . . . when he can. (*He puts down the phone.*)

JOY: (*off.*) Shall I send in Mr. Maples?

BILL: No. Get me Mrs. Eaves. Tell him I'm, tell him I'll be a couple of minutes. Now, get her quickly in case she's popped out. (*He waits. Very disturbed indeed. Buzz.*)

JOY: (*off.*) Mrs. Eaves.

BILL: Liz! Thank God: I thought you'd gone out. What? Do I? Well, I'll tell you, I'm sorry, but I just rung up old Winters. You know. . . . Well, he wouldn't speak to me. Which is all right, but he always speaks to me, even if it's only for half a minute, especially if I say it's urgent, which I did. And the funny thing is I *know* Hudson was with him. They swore he wasn't but he must have been. He couldn't have finished in the time. But old Winters and I have been quite pals. I must have put more work in his way over the past. . . . Exactly. . . . And he's a nice, straightforward . . . a bit brusque, but forthright. He even laughs at. . . . And then there was his clerk, Roberts. Charley Roberts. . . . I picked up the phone and I heard him say, I heard him say quite clearly 'Oh tell him I'm out or something. Anything'. He didn't even bother to lower his voice. It was like talking to you

89

now. . . . But, Charley. He's not like that. Bit
dull, like Hudson. But—he's just a posh office
boy. He's known me fifteen years. . . . But why
should he do that. . . . Well, sorry to bother
you. It was a just funny experience. . . . As soon
as we can—I'll ring you. Now, don't go out,
will you? Eh? Well, I'm seeing some kid for
importuning. That could take up a bit. . . .
Well, Jones has been doing it but he's obviously
muffed it, and I'll have to start more or less
. . . I *must* try and help. . . . Yes, perhaps too
hard, perhaps. . . . Well, I'm hoping Jane will
come in. . . . I'm just going to tell her that I
shan't be at her birthday weekend. That she
knows quite well it's because I'll be with you,
and that to please be honest with both of us,
and own up that she doesn't care whether I'm
there or not and that she's just letting herself be
used, or rather lending herself, as a blunt
instrument by her mother. . . . All right. . . .
Don't forget. . . .

(*He rings off.*)

JOY: (*off.*) Shall I——

BILL: Yes. And keep trying Winters. And tell them I
know Charley Roberts is there. . . . No, just
keep ringing. And when Mr. Hudson gets in,
tell him to come and see me right away.

JOY: O.K.

BILL: And say right away. Even if I have a client with
me.

JOY: Yes, Sir.

(*Presently she appears at the door and
announces*——)

JOY: Mr. Maples.

(JONES *comes in.* JONES—MAPLES *has some of*

90

JONES'S *unattractiveness but with other elements.*
In place of his puny arrogance and closed mind,
there is a quick-witted, improvising nature, not
without courage. His flashes of fear are like
bursts of creative energy, in contrast to JONES'S
whining fixity and confidence.

BILL: Mr. Maples. Sorry about all this waiting about
for you. I'm afraid it's. . . . Do sit down. No
calls, Joy. Right?

JOY: What about Mr. Winters?

BILL: Oh. Yes. Him.

JOY: And.

BILL: I don't know do I? Use your judgement. Well,
try me if you're not sure. But I must see to Mr.
Maples, I must see he's looked after. We *must*
get on with it.
(*Slight pause as he falters into another*
distraction. They watch him. He wrenches
himself out and dismisses her.)

BILL: All right.
(JOY *goes out.*)
Now, at last. So sorry. You've (*He looks for*
MAPLES' *file. Flips through papers.*) You've, yes,
you've been seeing—Mr. Jones.
(MAPLES *nods.*)
Yes, there's a fairly longish statement. And, of
course, a copy of your statement to the police.
And these other things. . . . It doesn't make a
very clear. . . at the moment, does it? Shall we
start more or less. . . .
(JOY *buzzes.*)

JOY: (*off.*) Your daughter's here.

BILL: Ask her to wait.

JOY: Only thing is she says she's not got very long.
Shall I——

91

BILL: Who has? Tell her to wait. Give her a cup of tea and discuss your teenage interests together.

JOY: I'm no teenager, thank you!

BILL: No one would know it. And look—don't let her go. She's got to stay and see me. After I'm through with Mr. Maples. Tell her that. (*Switches off.*) Fresh start was right. Yes, let me say to you——

(*He is thrown by the image of his daughter waiting outside. She is just visible to the audience.*)

As your lawyer, you have no, no obligations to me. Whatsoever. However, if you wish me to act in your interests, you should regard me like, the, the Queen, with the right to, to be consulted, to encourage and to warn I don't even ask for the truth. You may not be capable of it, it's difficult to retain for most of us, some of us at least, and when you're in a spot of trouble, as well, you are, let's be quite honest about it, and you feel you are gradually being deserted and isolated, it becomes elusive, more than ever, one can grasp so little, trust nothing, it's inhuman to be expected to be capable of giving a decent account of oneself. . . . Could you just shift your chair a little nearer to the desk. There, then I can see you properly. I hate to have my clients half way across the room, having to talk to themselves. Instead of to me. Shall we see if we can't find anything that's been left out. (*Pause.*) Who *are* you?

(*When* MAPLES *replies, his delivery adopts roughly the same style as in the* MRS. GARNSEY— ANDERSON—TONKS *dialogue.*)

92

MAPLES: How can I describe myself to you? I do seem
to be very ordinary, don't I?

BILL: I don't know. I wish I could see you more
clearly. This statement. . . .

MAPLES: Isn't true.

BILL: Well, I knew that before you came in.
(*Presently, he gives his evidence, like* BILL *himself
Mostly at speed, more polemic than reflection.*)

MAPLES: All right then. My name is John Montague,
after my uncle Monty, Maples. I am married, I
am quite young though I don't feel as if being
young ever happened to me. I've always been
married or in the army or living with my
parents. I have one child, aged six, a little girl,
Daphne, Susan, my wife's choice not mine. My
wife's name is Hilda. That was about the only
name she didn't need to be talked out of as she
hated it too. I met Hilda when I was still doing
my National Service, which was a bit of a
difficult time for me. But it isn't very interesting
to tell anyone because I don't have any proper
characteristics at all, save one, and there's not
even any interest in that, any more than there
is in being five feet seven or prone to hay
fever. Physically I'm lazy, on the whole, that
is, but it doesn't stop me being restless. I can't
stop at home, but most of the time I'm scared
to death of putting my nose outside the front
door. But sometimes I do. I'm there somehow,
on the, because of some row with Hilda, or
some excuse or I get back late from one of the
shops, and in twenty five minutes I'm in the
West End. I used to like to play tennis, which
I'm rather good at—And badminton, that too, I
played that at school. Hilda doesn't like anything

93

like that, and I haven't bothered. But I used to be rather good and full of energy and I could beat quite a lot of the others. There were always a few, though, and we used to have wonderful, great long duels when we should have been doing our homework. And it might even end up in a bit of a fight. A couple of times I even burst into tears when I was playing against someone called Shipley, his name was. He thought I was a bit mad, but it was all right. We were old friends. Nothing else. We talked about girls constantly, all the time.

(BILL *tries to take some of this in.* MAPLES *sees the effort and slows down the concentration for a few moments.*)

I'm sorry.

BILL: No. Go on.

MAPLES: Well, I met my wife, Hilda, while I was still in the Services.

BILL: Yes, I see. Let's see you're. . . .

MAPLES: I'm in the drapery business. My father-in-law's business actually, but I've done a bit about building it up. He had this old shop in Richmond, you see, ribbons, buttons, calico, towels, oh—cheap lot of old stuff. He'd have lost the lot in another year. Then Hilda and I got engaged, while I was still in the forces. There was nothing much I could think of to do then, I wanted. I'd got a pass 'O' level in G.C.E. but I didn't have a clue what to do with it. And I'd a sort of feeling for materials and I could organize a bit. I got rid of some of the old hags in the shop. Anyone could have done it, honestly. Anyway, now there's these three shops—the old one, one in Kingston and a new

one just opened up in Hounslow. I'd come back
late from Hounslow on this particular night.

BILL: Tell me about the arrest.

MAPLES: All right.

BILL: So I might as well throw this away.

MAPLES: I'll have to tell you about Denis.

BILL: Denis who? Oh, all right, tell me later.

MAPLES: Well, a year ago I nearly left Hilda. I fell in
love. I still think it was the first time. But I
couldn't bear the thought that I couldn't get
over it, that it was bigger than me, however
ordinary I might be. I never liked girls except
my sister but she wasn't always easy to talk to.
She could be suspicious and sort of
unwelcoming. We all talked about girls all the
time and we'd play games like seeing how we
could look up their skirts when they were
playing games or going upstairs on the bus.

BILL: I'll bet Shipley was good at that.

MAPLES: Yes. He was.

BILL: So was I, I'm afraid.

MAPLES: The only thing that excited me was playing
tennis, and especially the badminton with him.
I'd sweat for hours, before, during and
afterwards, and I couldn't get my homework
done in time for bed which scared me because
I was terrified of getting into trouble or being
found out in even little things, like not dubbining
my football boots or never understanding
what 'parsing' was. I never wanted to marry
Hilda or anyone else but I was scared stupid, I
was stupid anyway, not to. My mother was
always going on about the rottenest thing men
did was to get girls pregnant, which is what I
did, of course. So did my brother. But it didn't

95

matter for him. He's got three more now, and he's happy enough, and so's mother. No, I was never very fixed on her. My father's *much* nicer. Yes, I know you're thinking he was ineffectual and all that, but so was she, what was she so good at, at least he didn't scare anyone, or lean on anyone. He's all right. He maybe should have belted her across the chops a few times, but I doubt if anything or any of us could have changed. No, I never liked girls, but I didn't like men who didn't seem like men either. I think I believe in God. Still, I seem to let things happen to me. I have always let the others make the first advances, usually if it's possible in the dark, or with the lights turned down or something of that sort.

BILL: What about Hilda?

MAPLES: Oh, Hilda. We're getting on better.

BILL: And—she knows about this charge?

MAPLES: Oh yes. One of the detectives made a big point, coming round. We even had a drink together, the three of us by the end of it. *I* was offering him a drink. And he took it. But he knew what he was doing—*I* couldn't bribe anyone, not anywhere. I suppose you'll have to get up and say 'his wife is standing by him'.

BILL: Well it often makes a better impression in Court to say you're undergoing medical treatment.

MAPLES: Shall I tell you what the doctor said to me?

BILL: No. I've heard it. Did you get another doctor?

MAPLES: Yes. He agrees with *me*. But then he's the same. Just keep out of the law, keep out of the law and not to invite trouble. I don't want to change. I want to be who I am. But I stayed

96

with Hilda, I'd even given up Denis four months
ago, I hadn't spoken to him even for four
months and this happened. On the way back
from the new Hounslow shop. Hilda's mother
tries to call it a boutique, but I think I've talked
her out of that now. I used to have to get drunk,
first, like I did when I forced myself into bed
with Hilda and got married for it. But I haven't
had to do that for a long time. Do you think I
should plead guilty?

BILL: Not yet.

MAPLES: What's the advantage?

BILL: Of pleading guilty? It has the advantage of
certainty, that's all.

MAPLES: That sounds very attractive at the moment.

BILL: Well, I can't even guarantee that yet.
(JOY *buzzes*.)

JOY: I'm sorry, but your daughter wants to know how
much longer, because she can come back.

BILL: Tell her she's got to wait. I don't care. She's got
to wait. Now tell her (*Switches off.*) Can I offer
you anything?
(MAPLES *shakes his head.*)

MAPLES: Sometimes I would think I was unique, of
course. You know, years ago. I hoped I was.
But I'm not. I'm ordinary. But I wish I wasn't.
I didn't have a clue. Nothing happened until
after I was married, after Daphne was born.
For some reason I got on the wrong train, but
it was the right direction more or less and I just
stayed on it, standing up, all those bodies
pressed together and suddenly I felt two, maybe
three, fingers touch me, very lightly. Every time
the train stopped more people got out and there
was more room. I was scared to look up from

97

my paper and there wasn't any longer any excuse to be so close to anyone. A great draught of air came in from the platform and I felt cold, and it was Gunnersbury Station which is not too far from me, so I looked up and got out. I didn't dare look back but I heard the footsteps behind me. That was the first time and I'd had a few drinks first and I was very cold, at the back of some row of shops called something Parade, by the Midland Bank. About half past seven at night. That's about all I remember of it. When I got in, my dinner was all overcooked and simmering on a plate over the gas stove with the gravy gone hard round the edge of the plate, which is a bit like the way Hilda does things, spills them or upsets them or does them too much and she wasn't feeling well and couldn't get the baby to sleep. I went out into the garden, put my fingers down my throat and then buried it all with a trowel. If I wasn't married I'd have done it all the time, one to another, I suppose, but I don't think so. That's never been what I wanted. Oh, not that I haven't behaved. . . . They're right to get me, people like me. There was a young fellow, a sales manager at a store in Kingston. Do you know what I did? He was married. Nice girl. Rather attractive, not long married. Well, I set my sights and one night the three of us went out, got drunk, and while, all the time, while his wife was in the front——

BILL: Driving?——

MAPLES: Driving——

BILL: Actually in the back?

MAPLES: And she never knew. We were so damned

98

sharp, she never knew from beginning to end. Still doesn't know. Like Hilda, she never knew about Denis, about giving him up. I gave him up, you see. He wanted me to leave Hilda and take on a new life altogether. He begged me. He threatened to phone up or write to me. But he hasn't. He kept his promise. I longed to break the whole thing, and I think I would have done this particular night.

BILL: Do you still want to give him up?

MAPLES: No.

BILL: Do you think he's given you up?

(*Pause.*)

MAPLES: Yes. Probably. What's going to happen to me?

BILL: I don't know enough yet. I need to know more than that. I should think Sir Watkin Glover Q.C. is sure to apply the full rigour of the law and send the both of us down. What about the police?

MAPLES: I've only had one brush with the police before. Late one night by Turnham Green. He flashed his torch on us. He let the other one go, but he took my name and address and made me meet him the next night. Only about three times. I know you think I haven't tried. I can't make any more effort, any more, I want to plead guilty.

BILL: Well, you can't, now go on!

MAPLES: He asked me for a light, this policeman.

BILL: In plain clothes?

MAPLES: Naturally.

BILL: Look, try to help me, will you. Where?

MAPLES: Piccadilly Tube Station.

BILL: You're crazy.

MAPLES: I know. But I knew it was going to happen.

Sounds camp, but then the truth so often is. He was quite young, younger than I am, with lots of fair, wavy hair, like mine used to be, when I just went in the Army, before I met Hilda, before it started to go; he looked up. In the usual way. His eyes were pale and his cheekbones looked sharp and frail as if you could have smashed them with a knock from your finger, but when he walked away, you could see how really strong he must be. He walked straight into the cottage at number one entrance, you know, by the Regent Palace. And that was it. There was another one in there and they both of them grabbed me. Savile Row Station. Oh, quite gently. And no surprise to any of us. Denis and I had often talked about it happening. They seemed nice enough at first. I began to feel better and relaxed, as if I was being loved openly and attended on, and then, then the pressure turned on. What I ought to do. What the magistrate would say. What they knew. The one who had asked for the light had seen me with Denis. He said they knew all about him. About both of us. I had to keep him out of it. I knew nothing could be worse. So I, I signed this statement. And there it is. In front of you. So. Are you all right?

BILL: (*just audible.*) Yes.

MAPLES: You haven't taken anything down. Was it. . . .

BILL: Don't worry, we'll go through it all again with Hudson.

MAPLES: No. I don't think so.

BILL: You haven't seen me, my friend, you haven't seen me, cross-examining coppers is my speciality. But we'll get Winters in on this. Was

100

there anybody else there? It's a pity nobody saw
you.
(MAPLES *rises*.)

BILL: Joy! What's happening about Winters?

JOY: (*off.*) I tell you: I keep trying.

BILL: Well, Hudson'll be in soon. Tell him to come
straight in.
(*Switches off.*)
Don't move. It's only my daughter outside. It's
a pity about nobody seeing you. Oh, well—
perhaps there was.
(*Pause.*)
Don't worry—we'll get someone.
(*They look at each other.*)

MAPLES: Thank you. (*Pause.*) In the meantime, maybe
you'd better see your daughter.
(*He goes out. Presently* JANE *comes in.* BILL,
barely seeing her, waves her to the chair
MAPLES *has been sitting in. Slowly he takes her
in. He buzzes* JOY.)

BILL: Joy!

JOY: (*off.*) Well?

BILL: Joy.

JOY: (*off.*) Yes?

BILL: Don't let Mr. Maples go.

JOY: (*off.*) Well, I'm sorry——

BILL: All right. No. Wait.

JOY: (*sympathetically.*) (*off.*) Yes?

BILL: Get me another glass of water.
(*He looks across at his daughter. She fidgets.*)

BILL: (*slowly.*) You can wait just: one more minute—
(FADE.)
(FADE UP *on* JANE *and* BILL *together.* BILL'S
*speech must be started at the full flood. When he
fails it is with his longing. His daughter is cool,*

distressed, scared.

BILL: They're all pretending to ignore me. No
they're not pretending, they are! And that'll be
the going of you except that it's happened
already. Of course, it has, ages ago. Look at
me. Why you can't have looked at me and
seen anything, what, not for years, not since
you were a little tiny girl and I used to take you
out and hold your hand in the street. I always
used to think then that when you're the age
you are now, I'd take you out to restaurants for
dinner, big restaurants like I used to think posh
restaurants were like, with marble columns and
glass and orchestras. Like Lyons used to be
before you knew it. And I thought we'd behave
like a rather grand married couple, a bit casual
but with lots and lots of signals for one another.
And waves of waiters would pass in front of us
and admire us and envy us and we'd dance
together. (*holds her to him.*) Very slowly. (*pause.*)
And when we got back to our table, and when
it was all over, we'd lean forward and look at
each other with such, such oh, pleasure—we'd
hardly be able to eat our dinner. (*releases her.*)
So that when we got up, after a bit too much
champagne, we'd have to hang on to each other
very tightly indeed. And then: go home. . . I
always wish I'd been brought up in the country
you know. Won't be possible much longer.
There isn't any place for me, not like you. In
the law, in the country, or, indeed, in any place
in this city. My old father lives in the country,
as you know, but he doesn't want to see me these
days. Can't say I blame him. When I went to
see him the other day—whenever it was, do you

102

know, I tried to remind him of all sorts of
things we'd done together, but he simply
wouldn't, he wouldn't remember. And then the
old devil got mad and told me I was imagining
it. I had to go in the end. He was tired and he
wanted me to go. When I bent down and
kissed him, he didn't look up. . . . Your other
grandparents can hardly bring themselves to
acknowledge me. The old woman crossed to the
other side of the street once when I was pushing
you in the pram so as to avoid speaking to me.
Which surprised me. With you, I mean. They
have you over there and your mother goes, I
know, and they still give you generous presents
Christmas and birthday, but do you know when
they write to your mother, they never even
mention me by name, love to Bill, how's Bill,
nothing, not for ten years, and they only did it
in the early years after you were born because
they thought they had to if they were going to
be able to see you! And then they discovered
that they didn't even have to mime that genteel
little courtesy. How much do you think your
safety depends on the goodwill of others?
Well? Tell me. Or your safety? How safe do
you think you are? How? Safe?
(*She turns away increasingly frightened.*)
Do you want to get rid of me? Do *you*? Um?
Because I want to get rid of you.
(*She moves to the door.*)
(*toweringly cool for a while.*) Just a moment,
Jane. You can't go yet. Till I tell you. About
this famous weekend.
(*She shrugs impatiently.*)
Oh, I know it's none of your fault. But you

103

should know I shan't be with you, or, at least,
your mother then, just because I shall be with Liz
—a subject that bores you, I know, as much as
it's beginning to her, if you see—I'll be with her
for three whole days or something, if she'll have
me, I don't know that she will, but I'll be with
her instead of you on your seventeenth—is it
seventeen?—anyway, birthday and the reason
for that is because I know: that when I see you,
I cause you little else but distaste or distress, or,
at the least, your own vintage, swinging,
indifference. But nothing, certainly not your
swinging distaste can match what I feel for you.
(*Small pause as he changes tack*.) Or any of those
who are more and more like you. Oh, I read
about you, I see you in the streets. I hear what
you say, the sounds you make, the few jokes
you make, the wounds you inflict without even
longing to hurt, there is no lather or fear in you,
all cool, dreamy, young, cool and not a proper
blemish, forthright, unimpressed, contemptuous
of ambition but good and pushy all the same.
You've no shame of what you are, and, very
little, well, not much doubt as to what you'll
become. And quite right, at least so I used to
think. They're young, I said, and for the first
time they're being allowed to roll about in it
and have clothes and money and music and sex,
and you can take or leave any of it. No one
before has been able to do such things with
such charm, such ease, such frozen innocence as
all of you seem to have, to me. Only you, and
girls like you, naturally, could get on that
poor old erotic carthorse, the well known
plastic mac and manage to make it look pretty.

Pretty, mark you! Chic. Lively. You've stopped
its lumbering, indecent, slobbering ancient
longing and banged it into the middle of the
Daily Express—where they're only allowed to
say the word 'rape' if a black African's involved.
Or perhaps a nun. *You* don't even, not moved,
to wear make-up any longer. Your hair looks
like a Yorkshire terrier's come in from out of the
monsoon. And, yet, somehow, perversely, you
are more beautiful and certainly more dashing
than any of the girls I used to know and lust
after from morning to night, with their sweety,
tacky lipsticks and silk stockings on coupons
and permanent waves and thick hipped heavy
skirts. I don't know what you have to do with
me at all, and soon you won't, you'll go out of
that door and I'll not see you again. I am quite
sure of *that* by this time if nothing else. You
hardly drink except for some wine and pintfuls
of murky coffee. You'll go anywhere and more
or less seem to do anything, you've already
permanent sunless, bleached stains beneath your
breasts and two, likewise, crescents, on your
buttocks. You'll read any menu without
bothering, order what you want, and, what's
more, get it. Then maybe leave it. You'll hitch
hike and make your young noises from one
end of Europe to the other without a thought
of having the correct currency or the necessary
language. And you're right. And you dance
with each other, in such a way I, would never
have been able to master. (*He gazes longingly
across.*) But, and this is the but, I still don't
think what you're doing will ever, even, even,
even approach the fibbing, mumping, pinched

little worm of energy eating away in this me, of
mine, I mean. That is: which is that of being
slowly munched and then diminished altogether.
That worm, thank heaven, is not in your little
cherry rose. You are unselfconscious, which I
am not. You are without guilt, which I am not.
Quite rightly. Of course, you are stuffed full of
paltry relief for emergent countries, and marches
and boycotts and rallies, you, you kink your
innocent way along tirelessly to all that poetry
and endless jazz and folk worship, *and* looking
gay and touching and stylish all at the same
time. But there isn't much loving in any of your
kindnesses, Jane, not much kindness, not even
cruelty, really, in any of you, not much craving
for the harm of others, perhaps just a very easy,
controlled sharp, I mean 'sharp' pleasure in
discomfiture. You're flip and offhand and if you
are the unfeeling things you appear to be, no
one can really accuse you of being cruel in the
proper sense. If you should ever, and I hope you
shan't, my dear, I truly do for I've leapt at the
very idea of you, before you were ever born, let
alone the sight and smell of you; if you should
one day start to shrink slowly into an
unremarkable, gummy little hole into a world
outside the care or consciousness of anyone,
you'll have no rattlings of shame or death,
there'll be no little sweating, eruptions of blood,
no fevers or clots or flesh splitting anywhere or
haemorrhage. You'll have done everything well
and sensibly and stylishly. You'll know it
wasn't worth any candle that ever burned. You
will have to be blown out, snuffed, decently,
and not be watched spluttering and spilling and

hardening. You know what God is supposed to have said, well in Sunday School, anyway? God said, He said: Be fruitful and multiply and replenish the earth. And *subdue* it. It seems to me Jane, little Jane, you don't look little any longer, you are on your way at last, all, to doing all four of them. For the first time. Go on now. (*She waits. They elude each other. She goes out.*) (FADE.)

(FADE UP *on* BILL.)

BILL: Joy! Joy! What's going on out there? What? Joy! Where are you? What is it then? Joy! (JOY *enters in her overcoat.*)

JOY: So he's gone?

BILL: Oh, there you are. Who?

JOY: Hudson.

BILL: Yes.

JOY: Oh? Is he going to Piffards then?

BILL: Apparently.

JOY: I always thought he would.

BILL: So did I.

JOY: Well. . . .

BILL: Are you going home?

JOY: There's not much to stay for, is there?

BILL: I don't think so. Did you try Winters again before——

JOY: They've all gone home now. Which is where I should be. Is the Law Society really on to you?

BILL: Did Jones say so?

JOY: Yes.

BILL: Then I'm sure he's right.

JOY: Aren't you going to see Mrs. Eaves?

BILL: Do you know what a client said to me today?

JOY: No, who?

BILL: Oh, I don't know. One of them. She said when

I go out to the shops, I go to the ones furthest
away so that I can be out of the house and away
from him longer. Then I get angry when the
shopping is so heavy, and I can't carry it on my
own.

JOY: Crazy.

BILL: Stay a little longer.

JOY: What for?

BILL: Have a drink.

JOY: No thanks.

BILL: Well, stay and talk.

JOY: No.

BILL: I promised not to say 'please'.

JOY: What do you want me to do? Press myself in a
book for you? You know what? I think they're
all right. I don't like you either.

BILL: I know.

JOY: Well, I'm off. Like I should have done. . . .

BILL: I'm still surprised to hear you say it though. I
always am. And I shouldn't be. . . . Why does
it shock me? Why? I myself, am more packed
with spite and twitching with revenge than
anyone I know of. I actually often, frequently,
daily want to see people die for their errors. I
wish to kill them myself, to throw the switch
with my own fist. Fortunately, I've had no more
opportunities than most men. Still, I've made
more than the best of them. Will you come in
tomorrow?

JOY: I'll see.

BILL: Try to.

JOY: I have to take the day off.

BILL: Oh?

JOY: I've not been feeling so good lately. I think
maybe I need a bit of a rest.

BILL: I see.
    (LIZ *enters*.)
LIZ: Hullo.
JOY: Hullo, Mrs. Eaves.
LIZ: (*nods to* BILL.) How's your thumb?
BILL: Painful. A fat little tumour. On the end of another.
LIZ: In his usual state of catatonic immobility, are we?
BILL: Yes. (*to* JOY.) That's her way of saying I don't seem to be able to hold on, on to, to anything. She talks in that funny way because her father is a don and is what is called a conceptual thinker, which, it's all too clear, I am not. No, darling, it's not something in a rubber goods shop, it's what her father is. One of those little intellectual monkeys who chatter on the telly about Copernicus at two hundred words a minute. And don't ask me who Copernicus is. I don't know the name of the Prime Minister, at this moment. He's a very cold fish, Joy. Her father I mean. He's probably the only man living whose unconscious desires are entirely impersonal.
JOY: Well. I'll be off. Goodnight, Mrs. Eaves.
LIZ: Goodnight, Joy.
BILL: Goodnight.
JOY: 'Bye.
BILL: Joy.
    (*She goes out.* LIZ *goes over to him*.)
LIZ: My darling: are you all right?
BILL: Splendid.
LIZ: Why don't you come home?
BILL: Yes.
LIZ: I'm sorry, I had to come. You didn't answer the

telephone.

BILL: Didn't I?

LIZ: I wasn't interrupting anything was I?

BILL: No.

LIZ: Oh, come along. I don't know why you don't admit you knock off that girl——

BILL: Because I don't need to.

LIZ: I keep giving you opportunities.

BILL: Well, I don't want them. I don't want to be cued in by you——

LIZ: It's a lot to ask, you know.

BILL: Yes. I see that too.
(*Pause.*)

LIZ: You do ask a great deal of both of us, you know. It's unnecessary and it diminishes you.

BILL: True.

LIZ: I do love you.

BILL: Your assessment's impeccable. As usual.

LIZ: You're a dishonest little creep.

BILL: Why the 'little?' Because you seem to have more authority than I have. (*Pause.*) You're not *bigger*. You're cleverer. More accomplished, more generous. And more loving

LIZ: I've always managed to avoid guilt. It's a real peasant's pleasure, you know. For people without a sliver of self-knowledge or courage.

BILL: There *are* other qualities besides courage.

LIZ: Well?

BILL: Cowardice for instance. For example.

LIZ: I've not seen you since Thursday. I thought somehow we'd managed to resolve the pain of that particular evening. Even on the telephone.

BILL: So did I. So we did. Till the next time.

LIZ: I love you so dearly. I can't think what to say to you.

110

BILL: I think you will.

LIZ: Why can't you trust me? Please?

BILL: It isn't easy.

LIZ: I know.

BILL: It isn't easy to trust someone: you're busily betraying. Sit down. I can't see you over there. I don't like my clients sitting half way across the room talking to themselves.
(*She sits. Pause.*)

LIZ: What do you want to do?

BILL: Do?

LIZ: Yes, my darling. . . do.

BILL: I don't know. I haven't given it much thought.

LIZ: Did you see Jane?

BILL: Yes.

LIZ: How was that?
(*He looks at her.*)
I see. So. What's going to happen?

BILL: Liz!

LIZ: What!

BILL: I'm tired of being watched. I'm tired of being watched by you, and observed and scrutinized and assessed and guessed about.

LIZ: Who gives a damn!

BILL: You do, you did. But you won't.

LIZ: What are you saying? Do you want me to go—? Really?

BILL: Well, you're the one who insisted on what you called an ethic of frankness.

LIZ: Believe me, the last thing I would insist on is an ethic like that. I can't think of anything more destructive.
(*Phone rings.*)

BILL: Hullo. . . . No, everyone's gone.

LIZ: Well, we know who that is.

111

BILL: I'm just clearing up. . . . I told you, everyone's gone. . . . Just me. . . . Yes, she *is* here. . . . Because I couldn't be bothered to tell the truth . . . . Listen, now's not a very good time, is it? Look, I'll ring you back.

(*Pause.* LIZ *looks slightly mocking, but doesn't exploit it. She is too concerned for him.*)

When I leave you sometimes and I get in, deliberately, of course, about three or four a.m. and Anna's lying there in bed, pretending to be asleep. After making love to you and the drive back, I'm so tired and there's the following morning a couple of hours away only, but I pretend to sleep because I can't to begin with. We both just lie there. And if I'm lucky or drunk enough and I do go to sleep, she lies there choking in silence unable to sleep again till she wakes me in the morning. Do you know I can't remember one detail of what she looks like, not since I left this morning and we'd had the row about the weekend. I sat down to read the Charterhouse of Parma while you were away at Christmas. You said I'd like it. So I started. It took ten days and I gave up round about the middle somewhere. I can't tell you what it's about. I can't grasp anything. I used to be good at my job because I had what they called an instinct and a quick brain. Quick! I can't get through the Law reports. I leave everything to Hudson and now he's gone, and I wouldn't leave a camel's breakfast to Jones even if he *were* still here.

LIZ: Bill. What are we going to do?

BILL: Go away. I suppose.

LIZ: But where?

BILL: Far away, as far away as possible from this place. There's no place for me here.

LIZ: (*half humouring.*) I never think of you as a traveller.

BILL: Meaning?

LIZ: Well, you never seem to enjoy it much, do you? (*Pause.*) Well, do you?

BILL: Damn it, I've, I've travelled thousands of miles in the past few years for various clients in the last——

LIZ: Oh yes, flights to New York and Amsterdam and Geneva. They're just business men's bus rides.

BILL: What do you want then? What should I be? Lady Hester Stanhope with a briefcase of legal documents perched on a camel?

LIZ: I just don't think of your business trips as travel——

BILL: Oh, travel——

LIZ: They're just for getting from one place to another for a particular purpose.

BILL: (*bitterly.*) Well, what do *you* call travelling?

LIZ: Well, like, like going in a boat round the Isles of Greece.

BILL: Yes. With a lot of tight-lipped, fast-shooting dons on the look out for someone else's wife or crumpet.

LIZ: When you're anywhere, you're always desperately miserable. You want to get back.

BILL: Yes?

LIZ: Oh, to your clients. Or something. I was thinking, on my way here, and now. . . .

BILL: Well?

LIZ: I was thinking: perhaps you'd rather I didn't come away for the weekend.

113

(Silence. He faces her.)
I just thought you seemed . . . as if . . . you
might . . . want to be alone.
(Pause.)

BILL: I was only waiting, from the moment you came
in, for you to say that.

LIZ: I'm sorry to be so predictable. One often is,
you know, when someone knows you well and
loves you.

BILL: As I do. As I certainly do.

LIZ: I was trying my hardest to be honest. It's a
failing——

BILL: Well, why don't you take something for it.

LIZ: I don't care what you are or what you do——

BILL: Or who I am.

LIZ: I need you.

BILL: Not that word, please.

LIZ: You pretend to be ill and ignorant just so you
can escape reproach. You beggar and belittle
yourself just to get out of the game.

BILL: Whenever I do it, I enjoy, I think you do know,
being some, some sort of, sort of good and
comfort and pleasure to you because I love you.
I don't love you for the sake of that pleasure. I
can get it anywhere.
*(She touches his shoulder and kisses the back of
his head. He won't look up.)*

LIZ: You can always ring me.

BILL: But you won't be there.
(She can't reply.)
You do know that I love you?

LIZ: Yes.

BILL: And I shall never forget your face or anything
about you. It won't be possible. I think, I'm
quite certain, not that it matters, I loved you

114

more than anyone.

LIZ: More than Jane?

BILL: Yes.

LIZ: Goodbye.

(*She goes out.* BILL *takes a pill with a glass of water. He dials a number on the telephone.*)

BILL: Anna? Anna, what time is it? I can't see very clearly. . . . Do you think I should come home. . . . I don't think there's much point, do you? . . . Please don't cry, love. . . . I, I think it must be better if you don't see me . . . don't see me . . . yes . . . don't. Please don't don't. . . I'll have to put the receiver down. . . . I think I'll stay here. . . . Well the Law Society or someone will, sometime. . . . I think I'll just stay here. . . . Goodbye.

(*He replaces the receiver and sits back waiting.*)

CURTAIN

End of Play